Building Web Applications with Python and Neo4j

Develop exciting real-world Python-based web applications with Neo4j using frameworks such as Flask, Py2neo, and Django

Sumit Gupta

PUBLISHING

BIRMINGHAM - MUMBAI

Building Web Applications with Python and Neo4j

First published: July 2015

Production reference: 1100715

Published by Packt Publishing Ltd.
Livery Place
35 Livery Street
Birmingham B3 2PB, UK.

ISBN 978-1-78398-398-8

www.packtpub.com

Credits

Author
Sumit Gupta

Reviewers
Adarsh Deshratnam
Gianluca Tiepolo
Tsanyo Tsanev
Manuel Vives

Commissioning Editor
Kunal Parikh

Acquisition Editor
Larissa Pinto

Content Development Editor
Anish Sukumaran

Technical Editors
Novina Kewalramani
Ryan Kochery
Manal Pednekar

Copy Editors
Vikrant Phadke
Alpha Singh

Project Coordinator
Izzat Contractor

Proofreader
Safis Editing

Indexer
Rekha Nair

Production Coordinator
Aparna Bhagat

Cover Work
Aparna Bhagat

About the Author

Sumit Gupta is a seasoned professional, innovator, and technology evangelist, with over 100 months of experience in architecting, managing, and delivering enterprise solutions that revolve around a variety of business domains, such as hospitality, healthcare, risk management, insurance, and so on. He is passionate about technology, with over 14 years of hands-on experience in the software industry. Sumit has been using big data and cloud technologies for the past 4 to 5 years to solve complex business problems.

He is also the author of *Neo4j Essentials* (`http://neo4j.com/books/neo4j-essentials/`).

I want to acknowledge and express my gratitude to everyone who supported me in authoring this book. I am thankful for their inspiring guidance and valuable, constructive, and friendly advice.

About the Reviewers

Adarsh Deshratnam is a senior consultant (big data and cloud) whose focus is on designing, developing, and deploying Hadoop solutions for many MNCs. In this position, he has worked with customers to build several Hadoop applications with multiple database technologies, providing a unique perspective on moving customers beyond batch processing. An avid technologist, he focuses on technological innovations. Since 2006, he has been working full time and part time with big data and multiple database technologies. Adarsh completed his engineering at Staffordshire University with a computing major.

I would like to thank Packt Publishing for giving me the wonderful opportunity to review a book on one of the quickly evolving graph databases (Neo4j).

Gianluca Tiepolo has been programming since Windows 3.11 was around. As a cofounder of Sixth Sense Solutions, a start-up that is a global leader in retail solutions, he has worked with some of the world's biggest brands to deliver engaging, interactive experiences to their customers. He specializes in high-performance implementations of database services and computer vision. Currently, he's deeply involved in the open source community and has a lot of interest in big data.

I want to thank my wonderful wife, Adele; my awesome teammates; and my friend Marco for their support and inspiration.

Tsanyo Tsanev is a senior web developer at Dressler LLC in New York, USA. From the whiteboard to production, he has experience in building a variety of web applications. He began experimenting with Neo4j for the social networking website SongSilo and has since found many other uses for it. Tsanyo's passion is coding; he does it both for a living and as a hobby.

Manuel Vives is a software engineer, who focuses on Python and C++. He specializes in backend parts of distributed software and NoSQL databases. He used to work in France for a company that specializes in cybersecurity and training, and he now works in Canada.

www.PacktPub.com

Support files, eBooks, discount offers, and more

For support files and downloads related to your book, please visit www.PacktPub.com.

Did you know that Packt offers eBook versions of every book published, with PDF and ePub files available? You can upgrade to the eBook version at www.PacktPub.com and as a print book customer, you are entitled to a discount on the eBook copy. Get in touch with us at service@packtpub.com for more details.

At www.PacktPub.com, you can also read a collection of free technical articles, sign up for a range of free newsletters and receive exclusive discounts and offers on Packt books and eBooks.

https://www2.packtpub.com/books/subscription/packtlib

Do you need instant solutions to your IT questions? PacktLib is Packt's online digital book library. Here, you can search, access, and read Packt's entire library of books.

Why subscribe?

- Fully searchable across every book published by Packt
- Copy and paste, print, and bookmark content
- On demand and accessible via a web browser

Free access for Packt account holders

If you have an account with Packt at www.PacktPub.com, you can use this to access PacktLib today and view 9 entirely free books. Simply use your login credentials for immediate access.

Table of Contents

Preface

Relational databases have been one of the most widely used and most common forms of software systems for the storage of data since the 1970s. They are highly structured and store data in the form of tables, that is, with rows and columns. Structuring and storing data in the form of rows and columns has its own advantages; for example, it is easier to understand and locate data, reduce data redundancy by applying normalization, maintain data integrity, and much more.

But is this the best way to store any kind of data?

Let's consider an example of social networking:

Mike, John, and Claudia are friends. Claudia is married to Wilson. Mike and Wilson work for the same company.

Here is one of the possible ways to structure this data in a relational database:

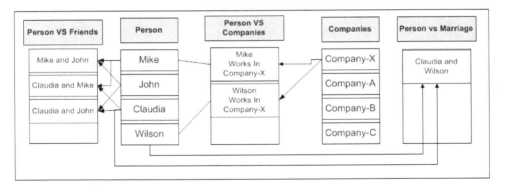

Complex, isn't it? And it can be more complex!

We should remember that relationships are evolving, and will evolve over a period of time. There could be new relationships, or there could be changes to existing relationships.

We can design a better structure but in any case, wouldn't that be forcibly fitting the model into a structure?

RDBMS is good for use cases where the relationship between entities is more or less static and does not change over a period of time. Moreover, the focus of RDBMS is more on the entities and less on the relationships between them.

There could be many more examples where RDBMS may not be the right choice:

1. Model and store 7 billion people objects and 3 billion non-people objects to provide an "earth view" drill-down from the planet to a sidewalk
2. Network management
3. Genealogy
4. Public transport links and road maps

Consider another way of modelling the same data:

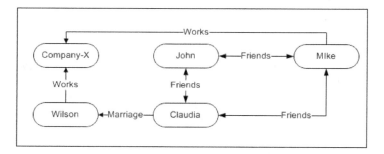

Simple, isn't it?

Welcome to the world of Neo4j—a graph database.

Although there is no single definition of graphs, here is the simplest one (`http://en.wikipedia.org/wiki/Graph_(abstract_data_type)`), which helps us to understand the theory of graphs:

> *A graph data structure consists of a finite (and possibly mutable) set of nodes or vertices, together with a set of ordered pairs of these nodes (or, in some cases, a set of unordered pairs). These pairs are known as edges or arcs. As in mathematics, an edge (x,y) is said to point or go from x to y. The nodes may be part of the graph structure, or may be external entities represented by integer indices or references.*

Neo4j, as an open source graph database, is part of the NoSQL family, and provides a flexible data structure, where the focus is on the relationships between the entities rather than the entities themselves.

Its first version (1.0) was released in February 2010, and since then, it has never stopped. It is amazing to see the pace at which Neo4J has evolved over the years. At the time of writing this book, the stable version was 2.2.RC01, which was released in March 2015.

If you are reading this book, then you probably already have sufficient knowledge about graph databases and Python. You will appreciate their contribution to the complex world of relationships.

Let's move forward and jump into the nitty-gritty of developing web applications with Python and Neo4j.

In the subsequent chapters, we will cover the various aspects dealing with data modelling, programming, and data analysis by means of application development with Python and Neo4j. We will cover the concepts of working with py2neo, Django, flask, and many more.

What this book covers

Chapter 1, Your First Query with Neo4j, details the process of the installation of Neo4j and Python on Windows and Linux. This chapter briefly explains the function of every tool installed together with Neo4j (shell, server, and browser). More importantly, it introduces, and helps you get familiar with, the Neo4j browser. You get to run the first basic Cypher query by using different methods exposed by Neo4j (shell, Java, the browser, and REST).

Chapter 2, Querying the Graph with Cypher, starts by explaining Cypher as a graph query language for Neo4j, and then we take a deep dive into the various Cypher constructs to perform read operations. This chapter also talks about the importance of patterns and pattern matching, and their usage in Cypher with various real-world and easy-to-understand examples.

Chapter 3, Mutating Graph with Cypher, starts by covering the Cypher constructs used to perform write operations on the Neo4j database. This chapter further talks about creating relationships between nodes and discusses the constraints required for maintaining the integrity of data. At the end, it discuss about the performance tuning of Cypher queries using various optimization techniques.

Chapter 4, Getting Python and Neo4j to Talk Py2neo, introduces Py2neo as a Python framework for working with Neo4j. This chapter explores various Python APIs exposed by Py2neo for working with Neo4j. It also talks about batch imports and introduces a social network use case, which is created and unit tested by using Py2neo APIs.

Chapter 5, Build RESTful Service with Flask and Py2neo, talks about building web applications and the integration of Flask and Py2neo. This chapter starts with the basics of Flask as a framework for exposing ReSTful APIs, and further talks about the Py2neo extension OGM (short for Object Graph Mapper) and its integration with Flask for performing various CRUD and search operations on the social network use case by creating and leveraging various ReST endpoints.

Chapter 6, Using Neo4j with Django and Neomodel, starts by describing Neomodel as an ORM for Neo4j. It discusses various high-level APIs exposed by Neomodel to perform CRUD and search operations using Python APIs or by directly executing Cypher queries. Finally, it talks about integration of two of the popular Python frameworks, Django and Neomodel.

Chapter 7, Deploying Neo4j in Production, explains the logical architecture of Neo4j, its various components, or APIs, such as filesystems, data organization and so on. Then we move on to the physical architecture of Neo4j, where we talk about meeting various NFRs imposed by typical enterprise deployments, such as HA, fault tolerance, data locality, backup, and recovery. Further, this chapter talks about various advanced Neo4j configurations and also discusses the various ways to monitor our Neo4j deployments.

What you need for this book

Readers should have programming experience in Python and some basic knowledge or understanding of any graph or NoSQL databases.

Who this book is for

This book is aimed at competent developers who have a good knowledge and understanding of Python that can allow efficient programming of the core elements and applications.

If you are reading this book, then you probably already have sufficient knowledge of Python. This book will cover data modelling, programming, and data analysis by means of application development with Python and Neo4j. It will cover concepts such as working with py2neo, Django, flask, and so on.

Conventions

In this book, you will find a number of text styles that distinguish between different kinds of information. Here are some examples of these styles and an explanation of their meaning.

Code words in text, database table names, folder names, filenames, file extensions, pathnames, dummy URLs, user input, and Twitter handles are shown as follows: "We can include other contexts through the use of the `include` directive."

A block of code is set as follows:

```
MATCH (x { name: "Bradley" })--(y)-->()
WITH x
CREATE (n:Male {name:"Smith", Age:"24"})-[r:FRIEND]->(x)
returnn,r,x;
```

Any command-line input or output is written as follows:

```
pip install flask Flask-RESTful
```

New terms and **important words** are shown in bold. Words that you see on the screen, for example, in menus or dialog boxes, appear in the text like this: "Now, click on the star sign in the panel on the extreme left-hand side, and click on **Create a node** in the provided menu."

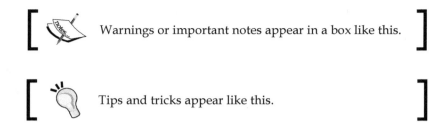

Warnings or important notes appear in a box like this.

Tips and tricks appear like this.

Reader feedback

Feedback from our readers is always welcome. Let us know what you think about this book—what you liked or disliked. Reader feedback is important for us as it helps us develop titles that you will really get the most out of.

To send us general feedback, simply e-mail feedback@packtpub.com, and mention the book's title in the subject of your message.

If there is a topic that you have expertise in and you are interested in either writing or contributing to a book, see our author guide at www.packtpub.com/authors.

Customer support

Now that you are the proud owner of a Packt book, we have a number of things to help you to get the most from your purchase.

Downloading the example code

You can download the example code files from your account at http://www.packtpub.com for all the Packt Publishing books you have purchased. If you purchased this book elsewhere, you can visit http://www.packtpub.com/support and register to have the files e-mailed directly to you.

Errata

Although we have taken every care to ensure the accuracy of our content, mistakes do happen. If you find a mistake in one of our books—maybe a mistake in the text or the code—we would be grateful if you could report this to us. By doing so, you can save other readers from frustration and help us improve subsequent versions of this book. If you find any errata, please report them by visiting http://www.packtpub.com/submit-errata, selecting your book, clicking on the **Errata Submission Form** link, and entering the details of your errata. Once your errata are verified, your submission will be accepted and the errata will be uploaded to our website or added to any list of existing errata under the Errata section of that title.

To view the previously submitted errata, go to https://www.packtpub.com/books/content/support and enter the name of the book in the search field. The required information will appear under the **Errata** section.

Piracy

Piracy of copyrighted material on the Internet is an ongoing problem across all media. At Packt, we take the protection of our copyright and licenses very seriously. If you come across any illegal copies of our works in any form on the Internet, please provide us with the location address or website name immediately so that we can pursue a remedy.

Please contact us at copyright@packtpub.com with a link to the suspected pirated material.

We appreciate your help in protecting our authors and our ability to bring you valuable content.

Questions

If you have a problem with any aspect of this book, you can contact us at questions@packtpub.com, and we will do our best to address the problem.

1
Your First Query with Neo4j

Neo4j is a graph database and has been in commercial development for over a decade. It comes with several flavors, supporting a wide variety of use cases and requirements imposed by start-ups, large enterprises, and Fortune 500 customers. It is a fully transactional database; it supports **Atomicity, Consistency, Isolation, Durability (ACID)** and is also well equipped to handle the complexities introduced by various kinds of systems—web-based, online transaction processing (OLTP), data-warehousing, analytics, and so on.

This chapter will help you to understand the paradigm, applicability, various aspects, and characteristics of Neo4j as a graph database. It will guide you through the installation process, starting right from downloading and running your first Cypher query leveraging various interfaces/tools/utilities exposed by Neo4j against your fully-working instance.

At the end of this chapter, your work environment will be fully functional, and you will be able to write your first Cypher query to insert/fetch the data from the Neo4j database.

This chapter will cover the following points:

- Thinking in graphs for SQL developers
- Licensing and configuring – Neo4j
- Using the Neo4j shell
- Introducing the Neo4j REST interface
- Running queries from the Neo4j browser

Thinking in graphs for SQL developers

Some might say that it is difficult for SQL developers to understand the paradigm of graphs, but it is not entirely true. The underlying essence of data modeling does not change. The focus is still on the entities and the relationship between these entities. Having said that, let's discuss the pros/cons, applicability, and similarity of the **relational models** and **graph models**.

The relational models are schema-oriented. If you know the structure of data in advance, it is easy to ensure that data conforms to it, and at the same time, it helps in enforcing stronger integrity. Some examples include traditional business applications, such as flight reservations, payroll, order processing, and many more.

The graph models are occurrence-oriented — Probabilistic model. They are adaptive and define a generic data structure that is evolving and works well with scenarios where the schema is not known in advance. The graph model is perfectly suited to store, manage, and extract highly-connected data.

Let's briefly discuss the disadvantages of the SQL databases, which led to the evolution of the graph databases:

- It is difficult to develop efficient models for evolving data, such as social networks
- The focus is more on the structure of data than the relationships
- They lack an efficient mechanism for performing recursions

All the preceding reasons were sufficient to design a different data structure, and as a result, the graph data structures were introduced.

The objective of the graph databases was specifically to meet the disadvantages of the SQL databases. However, Neo4j as a graph database, also leveraged the advantages of the SQL databases wherever possible and applicable. Let's see a few of the similarities between the SQL and graph databases:

- **Highly Consistent**: At any point in time, all nodes contain the same data at the same time
- **Transactional**: All insert or update operations are within a transaction where they are ACID

Having said that, it is not wrong to say that the graph databases are more or less the next generation of relational databases.

Comparing SQL and Cypher

Every database has its own query languages; for example, RDBMS leverages SQL and conforms to SQL-92 (http://en.wikipedia.org/wiki/SQL-92). Similarly, Neo4j also has its own query language—Cypher. The syntax of Cypher has similarities with SQL, though it still has its own unique characteristics, which we will discuss in the upcoming sections.

Neo4j leveraged the concept of patterns and pattern matching, and introduced a new declarative graph query language, Cypher, for the Neo4j graph database. Patterns and pattern matching are the essence and core of Neo4j, so let's take a moment to understand them. We will then talk about the similarities between SQL and Cypher.

Patterns are a given sequence or occurrence of tokens in a particular format. The act of matching patterns within a given sequence of characters or any other compatible input form is known as pattern matching. Pattern matching should not be confused with pattern recognition, which usually produces the exact match and does not have any concept of partial matches.

Pattern matching is the heart of Cypher and a very important component of the graph databases. It helps in searching and identifying a single or a group of nodes by walking along the graph. Refer to http://en.wikipedia.org/wiki/Pattern_matching for more information on the importance of pattern matching in graphs. Let's move forward and talk about Cypher, and it's similarities with SQL.

Cypher is specifically designed to be a human query language, which is focused on making things simpler for developers. Cypher is a declarative language and implements "What to retrieve" and not "how to retrieve", which is in contrast to the other imperative languages, such as Java and Gremlin (refer to http://gremlin.tinkerpop.com/).

Cypher borrows much of its structure from SQL, which makes it easy to use/ understand for SQL developers. "SQL familiarity" is another objective of Cypher.

Let's refer to the following illustration, which defines the Cypher constructs and the similarity of Cypher with SQL constructs:

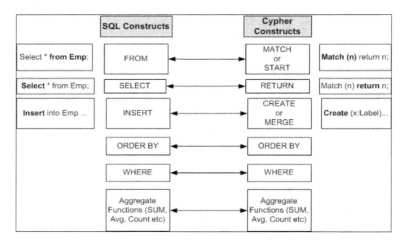

The preceding diagram defines the mapping of the common SQL and Cypher constructs. It also depicts the examples stating the usage of these constructs.

For instance, FROM is similar to MATCH or START and produces the same results. Although the way they are used is different but the objective and concept remains the same.

We will talk about Cypher in detail in *Chapter 2, Querying the Graph with Cypher* and *Chapter 3, Mutating Graph with Cypher,* but without getting into the nitty-gritty and syntactical details. The following is one more illustration that briefly describes the similarities between the Cypher and SQL constructs:

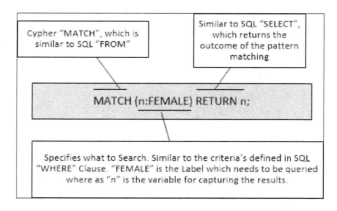

In the preceding illustration, we are retrieving the data using Cypher pattern matching. In the statement shown in the preceding diagram, we are retrieving all the nodes that are labeled with FEMALE in our Neo4j database. This statement is very similar to the SQL statement where we want to retrieve some specific rows of a table based on a given criteria, such as the following query:

```
SELECT * from EMPLOYEE where GENDER = 'FEMALE'
```

The preceding examples should be sufficient to understand that SQL developers can learn Cypher in no time.

Let's take one more example where we want to retrieve the total number of employees in the company X:

- **SQL syntax**: Select count (EMP-ID) from Employee where COMPANY_ NAME='X'

- **Cypher syntax**: match (n) where n.CompanyName='X' return count(n);

The preceding Cypher query shows the usage of aggregations such as count, which can also be replaced by sum, avg, min, max, and so on.

 Refer to http://neo4j.com/docs/stable/query-aggregation. html for further information on aggregations in Cypher.

Let's move forward and discuss the transformation of the SQL data structures into the graph data structures.

Evolving graph structures from SQL models

The relational models are the simplest models to depict and define the entities and the relationship between those entities. It is easy to understand and you can quickly whiteboard with your colleagues and domain experts.

A graph model is similar to a relational model as both models are focused on the domain and use case. However, there is a substantial difference in the way they are created and defined. We will discuss the way the graph models are derived from the relational models, but before that, let's look at the important components of the graph models:

- **Nodes**: This component represents entities such as people, businesses, accounts, or any other item you might want to keep track of.

- **Labels**: This component is the tag that defines the category of nodes. There can be one or more labels on a node. A label also helps in creating indexes, which further help in faster retrievals. We will discuss this in *Chapter 3, Mutating Graph with Cypher*.
- **Relationship**: This component is the line that defines the connection between the two nodes. Relationship can further have its own properties and direction.
- **Properties**: This component is pertinent information that relates to the nodes. This can be applied to a node or the relationship.

Let's take an example of a relational model, which is about an organization, and then understand the process of converting this into a graph model:

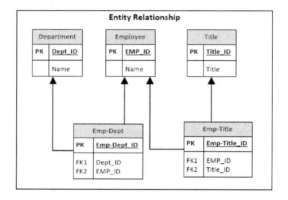

In the preceding relational model, we have employee, department, and title as entities, and `Emp-Dept` and `Emp-Title` as the relationship tables.

Here is sample data within this model:

Employee				Department			Title	
EMP_ID	Name	Age		DEPT_ID	Name		Title_ID	Title
E-101	John	45		X-105	Admin		T-1	Supervisor
							T-2	CEO

EMP-DEPT				Emp_Title		
EMP-DEPT_ID	DEPT_ID	EMP_ID		EMP-Title_ID	EMP_ID	Title_ID
ED-1	X-105	E-101		ET-1	E-101	T-2

The preceding screenshot depicts the sample data within the relational structures. The following are the guidelines to convert the preceding relational model into the graph model:

- The entity table is represented by a label on nodes
- Each row in an entity table is a node
- The columns on these tables become the node properties
- The foreign keys and the join tables are transformed into relationships; columns on these tables become the relationship properties

Now, let's follow the preceding guidelines and convert our relational model into the graph model, which will look something like the below image:

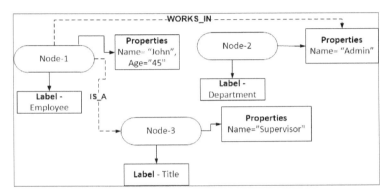

The preceding illustration defines the complete process and the organization of data residing in the relational models into the graph models. We can use the same guidelines for transforming a variety of relational models into the graph structures.

In this section, we discussed the similarities between SQL and Cypher. We also talked and discussed about the rules and processes of transforming the relational models into graph models. Let's move forward and understand the licensing and installation procedure of Neo4j.

Licensing and configuring – Neo4j

Neo4j is an open source graph database, which means all its sources are available to the public (currently on GitHub at `https://github.com/neo4j/neo4j`). However, Neo Technology, the company behind Neo4j, distributes the latter in two different editions—the Community edition and Enterprise edition. Let's briefly discuss the licensing policy for the Community and Enterprise editions, and then we will talk about the installation procedures on the Unix/Linux operating systems.

Licensing – Community Edition

Community Edition is a single node installation licensed under **General Public License (GPL)** Version 3 (`http://en.wikipedia.org/wiki/GNU_General_Public_License`) and is used for the following purposes:

- Preproduction environments, such as development or QA for fast paced developments
- Small to medium scale applications where it is preferred to embed the database within the existing application
- Research and development where advanced monitoring and high performance is not the focus

You can benefit from the support of the whole Neo4j community on Stack Overflow, Google Groups, and Twitter.

 If you plan to ask a question on Stack Overflow, do not forget to tag your question with the #Neo4j hashtag.

Licensing – Enterprise Edition

Enterprise Edition comes with three different kinds of subscription options and provides the distributed deployment of the Neo4j databases, along with various other features, such as backup, recovery, replication, and so on.

- **Personal license**: It is free of charge and may look very similar to Community Edition. It targets students, as well as small businesses.

- **Startup program**: Starting from this plan, you can benefit from the enterprise support. A startup license allows workday support hours — 10 hours per 5 business days.

- **Enterprise subscriptions**: With this plan, you can benefit from 24/7 support and emergency custom patches if needed. At this scale, your company will have to directly contact Neo Technology to assess the cost of your required setup.

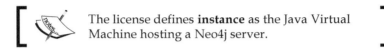

The license defines **instance** as the Java Virtual Machine hosting a Neo4j server.

Each of the subscription is subject to its own license and pricing. Visit `http://neo4j.com/subscriptions/` for more information about available subscriptions with Enterprise Edition.

Installing Neo4J Community Edition on Linux/Unix

In this section, we will talk about the Neo4j installation on the Linux/Unix operating system. At the end of this section, you will have a fully-functional Neo4j instance running on your Linux/Unix desktop/server.

Let's perform the following common steps involved in the Neo4j installation on Linux/Unix:

1. Download and install Oracle Java 7 (`http://www.oracle.com/technetwork/java/javase/install-linux-self-extracting-138783.html`) or open JDK 7 (`https://jdk7.java.net/download.html`).

2. Set `JAVA_HOME` as an environment variable and the value of this variable will be the file system path of your JDK installation directory:

   ```
   export JAVA_HOME=<Path of Java install Dir>
   ```

3. Download the stable release of the Linux distribution, neo4j-community-2.2.0-RC01-unix.tar.gz, from http://neo4j.com/download/other-releases/.

Neo4j Release	Community	Enterprise
	Neo4j 2.1.7 3 February 2015 Release Notes | Read More	
Linux/Mac	Neo4j 2.1.7	Neo4j 2.1.7
Windows 64 bit	Neo4j 2.1.7 (exe) | Neo4j 2.1.7 (zip)	Neo4j 2.1.7 (zip)
Windows 32 bit	Neo4j 2.1.7 (exe) | Neo4j 2.1.7 (zip)	Neo4j 2.1.7 (zip)
	Neo4j 2.2 RC01 – Release Candidate *For Development Only* 5 March, 2015	
Linux/Mac	Neo4j 2.2.0-RC01	Neo4j 2.2.0-RC01
Windows 64 bit	Neo4j 2.2.0-RC01 (exe) | Neo4j 2.2.0-RC01 (zip)	Neo4j 2.2.0-RC01 (zip)
Windows 32 bit	Neo4j 2.2.0-RC01 (exe) | Neo4j 2.2.0-RC01(zip)	Neo4j 2.2.0-RC01 (zip)

Neo4j can be installed and executed as a Linux service, or it can also be downloaded as the .tar file, where, after installation, it needs to be started manually.

Let's talk about the steps involved in installing Neo4j as a service, and then we will also talk about the standalone archive.

Installing as a Linux tar / standalone application

Architects have always preferred to install critical applications as a Linux service, but there can be reasons, such as insufficient privileges, which restrict you from installing software as a Linux service. So, whenever you cannot install software as a Linux service, there is another way in which you can download Neo4j, perform manual configuration, and start using it.

Let's perform the following steps to install Neo4j as a Linux tar / standalone application:

1. Once you have downloaded the Neo4j archive, browse the directory from where you want to extract the Neo4j server and untar the Linux/Unix archive: tar -xf <location of Archive file>. Let's refer to the top-level extracted directory as $NEO4J_HOME.

2. Open the Linux shell or console and execute the following commands for starting the sever:

   ° <$NEO4J_HOME>/bin/neo4j - start: This command is used for running the server in a new process

- ° `<$NEO4J_HOME>/bin/neo4j - console`: This command is used for running the server in the same process or window without forking a new process
- ° `<$NEO4J_HOME>/bin/neo4j - restart`: This command is used for restarting the server

3. Browse `http://localhost:7474/browser/` and you will see the login screen of the Neo4j browser.

4. Enter the default username/password as `neo4j/neo4j` and press *Enter*. The next screen will ask you to change the default password.

5. Change the password and make sure that you remember it. We will use this new password in the upcoming examples.

6. Stop the server by pressing *Ctrl* + *C* or by typing `<$NEO4J_HOME>/bin/neo4j - stop`.

Installing as a Linux service

This is the most preferred procedure for installing Neo4j in all kinds of environments, whether it's production, development, or QA. Installing Neo4j as a Linux service helps a Neo4j server and database to be available for use at server start-up and also survive user logons/logoffs. It also provides various other benefits such as ease of installation, configuration, and up-gradation.

Let's perform the following steps and install Neo4j as a Linux service:

1. Once the Neo4j archive is downloaded, browse the directory from where you want to extract the Neo4j server and untar the Linux/Unix archive: `tar -xf <location of Archive file>`. Let's refer to the top-level extracted directory as `$NEO4J_HOME`.

2. Change the directory to `$NEO4J_HOME`; and execute the command, `sudo bin/neo4j neo4j-installer install`; and follow the steps as they appear on the screen.

> The installation procedure will provide an option to select the user that will be used to run the Neo4j server. You can supply any existing or new Linux user (defaults to Neo4j). If a user is not present, it will be created as a system account and the ownership of `<$NEO4J_HOME>/data` will be moved to that user.

3. Once the installation is successfully completed, execute `sudo service neo4j-service start` on the Linux console for starting the server and `sudo service neo4j-service stop` for gracefully stopping the server.

4. Browse `http://localhost:7474/browser/` and you will see the login screen of the Neo4j browser.

5. Enter the default username/password as `neo4j/neo4j` and press *Enter*. The next screen will ask you to change the default password.

6. Change the password and make sure that you remember it. We will use this new password in the upcoming examples.

 To access the Neo4j browser on remote machines, enable and modify `org.neo4j.server.webserver.address` in `neo4j-server.properties` and restart the server.

Installing Neo4j Enterprise Edition on Unix/Linux

High availability, fault tolerance, replication, backup, and recovery are a few of the notable features provided by Neo4j Enterprise Edition. Setting up a cluster of Neo4j nodes is quite similar to the single node setup, except for a few properties which need to be modified for the identification of node in a cluster.

Let's perform the following steps for installing Neo4j Enterprise Edition on Linux:

1. Download and install Oracle Java 7 (`http://www.oracle.com/technetwork/java/javase/install-linux-self-extracting-138783.html`) or open JDK 7 (`https://jdk7.java.net/download.html`).

2. Set `JAVA_HOME` as the environment variable and the value of this variable will be the file system path of your JDK installation directory:

   `export JAVA_HOME=<Path of Java install Dir>`

3. Download the stable release of the Linux distribution, `neo4j-community-2.2.0-RC01-unix.tar.gz` from `http://neo4j.com/download/other-releases/`.

4. Once downloaded, extract the archive into any of the selected folders and let's refer to the top-level extracted directory as `$NEO4J_HOME`.

5. Open `<$NEO4J_HOME>\conf\neo4j-server.properties` and enable/modify the following properties:

   ○ `org.neo4j.server.database.mode=HA`: Keep this value as `HA`, which means **high availability**. You can run it as a standalone too by providing the value as `SINGLE`.

   ○ `org.neo4j.server.webserver.address=0.0.0.0`: This property enables and provides the IP of the node for enabling remote access.

6. Open `<$NEO4J_HOME>\conf\neo4j.properties` and enable/modify the following properties:

   ○ `ha.server_id=`: This property is the unique ID of each node that will participate in the cluster. It should be an integer (1, 2, or 3).

   ○ `ha.cluster_server=192.168.0.1:5001`: This property is the IP address and port for communicating the cluster status information with other instances.

   ○ `ha.server=192.168.0.1:6001`: This property is the IP address and port for the node for communicating the transactional data with other instances.

   ○ `ha.initial_hosts=192.168.0.1:5001,192.168.0.2:5001`: This property is a comma-separated list of `host:port` (`ha.cluster_server`) where all nodes will be listening. This will be the same for all the nodes participating in the same cluster.

   ○ `remote_shell_enabled=true`: Enable this property for connecting the server remotely through the shell.

   ○ `remote_shell_host=127.0.0.1`: This property enables and provides an IP address where remote shell will be listening.

   ○ `remote_shell_port=1337`: This property enables and provides the port at which shell will listen. You can keep it as default in case the default port is not being used by any other process.

7. Open `<$NEO4J_HOME>/bin`, execute `./neo4j start` and you are done. Stop the server by pressing *Ctrl + C* or by typing `./neo4j stop`.

8. Browse `http://<IP>:7474/browser/` for interactive shell, and on the login screen, enter the default username/password as `neo4j/neo4j` and press *Enter*.

9. The next screen will ask you to change the default password. Change the password and make sure that you remember it. We will use this new password in the upcoming examples.

Using the Neo4j shell

The Neo4j shell is a powerful interactive shell for interacting with the Neo4j database. It is used for performing the CRUD operations on graphs.

The Neo4j shell can be executed locally (on the same machine on which we have installed the Neo4j server) or remotely (by connecting the Neo4j shell to a remote sever).

By default, the Neo4j shell (`<$NEO4J_HOME>/bin/neo4j-shell`) can be executed on the same machine on which the Neo4j server is installed, but the following configuration changes are required in `<$NEO4J_HOME>/conf/neo4j.properties` to enable the connectivity of the Neo4j database from the remote machines:

- `remote_shell_enabled=true`: This configuration enables the property
- `remote_shell_host=127.0.0.1`: This configuration enables and provides the IP address of the machine on which the Neo4j server is installed
- `remote_shell_port=1337`: This configuration enables and defines the port for incoming connections

Let's talk about various other options provided by the Neo4j shell for connecting to the local Neo4j server:

- `neo4j-shell -path <PATH>`: This option shows the path of the database directory on the local file system. A new database will be created in case the given path does not contain a valid Neo4j database.
- `neo4j-shell -pid <PID>`: This option connects to a specific process ID.
- `neo4j-shell -readonly`: This option connects to the local database in the READ ONLY mode.
- `neo4j-shell -c <COMMAND>`: This option executes a single Cypher statement and then the shell exits.
- `neo4j-shell -file <FILE >`: This option reads the contents of the file (multiple Cypher CRUD operations), and then executes it.
- `neo4j-shell —config - <CONFIG>`: This option reads the given configuration file (such as `neo4j-server.properties`) from the specified location, and then starts the shell.

The following are the options for connecting to the remote Neo4j server:

- `neo4j-shell -port <PORT>`: This option connects to the server running on a port different to the default port (1337)
- `neo4j-shell -host <HOST>`: This option shows the IP address or domain name of the remote host on which the Neo4j server is installed and running.

Let's move forward and get our hands dirty with the system.

To begin with and to make it simple, first we will insert the data, and then try to fetch the same data through the Neo4j shell.

Let's perform the following steps for running our Cypher queries in the Neo4j shell:

1. Open your UNIX shell/console and execute `<$NEO4J_HOME>/bin/neo4j start`. This will start your Neo4j server in another process.

2. In the same console, execute `<$NEO4J_HOME>/bin/neo4j-shell` to start the Neo4j shell.

3. Next, execute the following set of statements on the console:

   ```
   CREATE (movies:Movie {Name:"Noah", ReleaseYear:"2014"});
   MATCH (n) return n;
   MATCH (n) delete n;
   ```

4. You will see something like the following image on your console:

```
neo4j-sh (?)$ CREATE (movies:Movie {Name:"Noah", ReleaseYear:"2014"});
+-------------------+
| No data returned. |
+-------------------+
Nodes created: 1
Properties set: 2
Labels added: 1
22 ms
neo4j-sh (?)$ MATCH (n) return n;
+---------------------------------------------+
| n                                           |
+---------------------------------------------+
| Node[5]{Name:"Noah",ReleaseYear:"2014"}     |
+---------------------------------------------+
1 row
24 ms
neo4j-sh (?)$ MATCH (n) delete n;
+-------------------+
| No data returned. |
+-------------------+
Nodes deleted: 1
44 ms
neo4j-sh (?)$
```

Yes, that's it...we are done!

We will dive deep into the details of the Cypher statements in the upcoming chapters, but let's see the results of each of the preceding Cypher statements:

- `CREATE (movies:Movie {Name:"Noah", ReleaseYear:"2014"});`: This statement creates a node with two attributes, `Name:"Noah"` and `ReleaseYear:"2014"`, and a label, `Movie`

- `MATCH (n) return n;`: This statement searches the Neo4j database and prints all the nodes and their associated properties on the console

- `MATCH (n) delete n;`: This statement searches the Neo4j database and deletes all the selected nodes

Introducing the Neo4j REST interface

Neo4j exposes a variety of REST APIs for performing the CRUD operations. It also provides various endpoints for the search and graph traversals. Neo4j 2.2.x provides the additional feature of securing the REST endpoints.

Let's move forward and see a step-by-step process to access and execute the REST APIs for performing the CRUD operations.

Authorization and authentication

In order to prevent unauthorized access to endpoints, Neo4j 2.2.x, by default, provides token-based authorization and authentication for all the REST endpoints.

Therefore, before running any CRUD operations, we need to get the security token so that every request is authenticated and authorized by the Neo4j server.

Let's perform the following steps for getting the token:

1. Open your UNIX shell/console and execute `<$NEO4J_HOME>/bin/neo4j start` to start your Neo4j server, in case it is not running.

2. Download any tool such as SOAP-UI (`http://www.soapui.org/`), which provides the creation and execution of the REST calls.

3. Open your tool and execute the following request and parameters for creating data in the Neo4j database:
   - **Request method type**: `POST`
   - **Request URL**: `http://localhost:7474/authentication`
   - **Request headers**: `Accept: application/json; charset=UTF-8` and `Content-Type: application/json`
   - **Additional HTTP header**: `Authorization= Basic <base64(username:password)>`

4. In the preceding request, replace `<base64(username:password)>` with the `base64` encoded string for `username:password`. This username is the default username, `neo4j`, and the password is the real password, which was provided/changed when you accessed your Neo4j browser for the first time.

5. For example, the `base64` encoded string for username, `neo4j`, and password, `sumit`, will be `bmVvNGo6c3VtaXQ=`, so now your additional HTTP header will be something like the following:

   ```
   Authorization = Basic bmVvNGo6c3VtaXQ=
   ```

The preceding screenshot shows the format of the request along with all the required parameters for authorizing the REST-based request to the Neo4j server.

You can also switch off the authentication by modifying `dbms.security.authorization_enabled=true` in `$NEO4J_HOME/conf/neo4j-server.propoerties`. Restart your server after modifying the property.

Now, as we have a valid token, let's move ahead and execute various CRUD operations.

 For converting in `base64`, you can use the online utility at `http://www.motobit.com/util/base64-decoder-encoder.asp` or you can also use the Python `base64` library at `https://docs.python.org/2/library/base64.html`.

CRUD operations

Create, read, update, and delete are the four basic and most common operations for any persistence storage. In this section, we will talk about the process and syntax leveraged by Neo4j to perform all these basic operations.

Perform the following steps for creating, searching, and deleting data in the Neo4j database:

1. Download any tool such as SOAP-UI (`http://www.soapui.org/`), which provides the creation and execution of the REST calls.

2. Open your tool and execute the following request and parameters for creating data in the Neo4j database:

   ◦ **Request method type**: POST

   ◦ **Request URL**: `http://localhost:7474/db/data/transaction`

   ◦ **Request headers**: `Accept: application/json; charset=UTF-8` and `Content-Type: application/json`

- ° **JSON-REQUEST**: {"statements": [{"statement" : "CREATE (movies:Movie {Name:"Noah", ReleaseYear:"2014"});"}]}
- ° **Additional HTTP header**: Authorization = Basic <base64(username:password)>

3. Replace <base64(username:password)> with the actual base64 token, which we generated in the *Authorization and Authentication* section, and execute the request. You will see no errors and the output will look something like the following screenshot:

In the preceding screenshot, the CREATE request created a label Movie with two attributes, Name and ReleaseYear

4. Next, let's search the data, which we created in the previous example. Open your tool and execute the following request and parameters for searching data in the Neo4j database:
   - ° **Request method type**: POST
   - ° **Request URL**: http://localhost:7474/db/data/transaction
   - ° **Request Headers**: Accept: application/json; charset=UTF-8 and Content-Type: application/json
   - ° **JSON-REQUEST**: {"statements": [{"statement" : "MATCH (n) return n;"}]}
   - ° **Additional HTTP Header**: Authorization = Basic <base64(username:password)>

5. Replace `<base64(username:password)>` with the actual `base64` token, which we generated in the *Authorization and Authentication* section and execute the request. You will see no errors and the output will look something like the following screenshot:

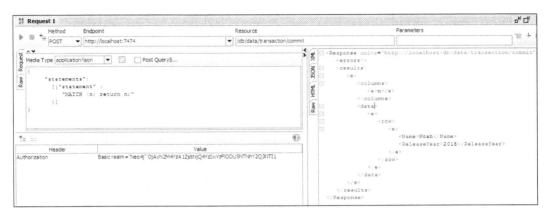

In the preceding screenshot, the MATCH request searched the complete database and returned all the nodes and their associated properties.

6. Next, let's delete the data, which we searched in the preceding step. Open your tool and execute the following request and parameters for search, and then delete the data from the Neo4j database in a single Cypher statement:

   ○ **Request method type**: POST

   ○ **Request URL**: `http://localhost:7474/db/data/transaction/commit`

   ○ **Request headers**: `Accept: application/json; charset=UTF-8` and `Content-Type: application/json`

   ○ **JSON-REQUEST**: `{"statements": [{"statement" : "MATCH (n) delete n;"}]}`

   ○ **Header-Parameter**: `Authorization = Basic realm="Neo4j" <BASE64-ENCODED-TOKEN>`

7. Replace `<BASE64-ENCODED-TOKEN>` with the actual `base64` token, which we generated in the *Authorization and Authentication* section, and execute the request. The response of the `delete` request will be same as the `Create` request.

In this section, we walked through the process of executing the Cypher queries with one of the REST endpoints, `/db/data/transaction/commit`, which is known as **Transactional Cypher HTTP Endpoint**. There are various other REST endpoints exposed by Neo4j for performing traversals, search, CRUD, administration, and a health check of the Neo4j server. Refer to `http://neo4j.com/docs/stable/rest-api.html` for a complete list of available endpoints, or you can also execute another REST point exposed by Neo4j, `/db/data`, which is known as the `service root` and the starting point to discover the REST API. It contains the basic starting points for the database along with some version and extension information.

 Linux users can also use the `curl` command to create and retrieve the data using the Neo4j REST APIs (`http://neo4j.com/blog/the-neo4j-rest-server-part1-get-it-going/`).

Running queries from the Neo4j browser

In the previous sections, we saw the results of our Cypher queries in the console (the Neo4j console) and JSON (REST) format, but both of these formats do not provide enough visualization. Also, as data grows, it becomes even more difficult to analyze the nodes and their relationships.

How about having a rich user interface for visualizing data in a graph format – a series of connected nodes? It will be awesome…correct?

Neo4j provides a rich graphical and interactive user interface for fetching and visualizing the Neo4j graph data, the **Neo4j browser**. The Neo4j browser not only provides the data visualization, but, at the same time, it also provides insights into the health of the Neo4j system and its configurations.

Let's perform the following steps for executing a Cypher search query from our Neo4j browser, and then visualize the data:

1. Assuming that your Neo4j server is running, open any browser such as IE, Firefox, Mozilla, or Safari on the same system on which your Neo4j server is installed, and enter the URL, `http://localhost:7474/browser` in the browser navigation bar. Now press *Enter*.

2. Next, enter the server username and password on the login screen (which we created/changed during the Neo4j installation), and click **Submit**.

3. Now, click on the star sign in the panel on the extreme left-hand side, and click **Create a node** from the provided menu.

4. Next, enter the following Cypher query to create data in the box provided below the browser's navigation bar (besides $): `CREATE (movies:Movie {Name:"Noah", ReleaseYear:"2014"});`. Now click on the right arrow sign at the extreme right corner, just below the browser's navigation bar.

5. Click on **Get some data** from the panel on the left-hand side, and execute the following Cypher query to retrieve the data from the Neo4j database: `"MATCH (n) return n;`. You will see the following results:

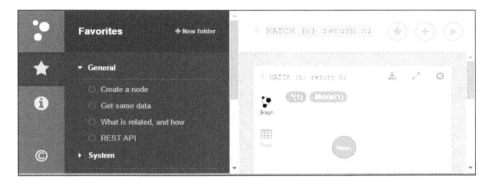

And we are done! You can also execute the REST APIs by clicking on the **REST API** or see the relationships by clicking on **What is related, and how**.

There are many other rich, interactive, and intuitive features of the Neo4j browser. For the complete list of features, execute `:play intro` in the same window where you executed your Cypher query and it will walk you through the various features of the Neo4j browser.

Summary

In this chapter, we learned about the similarity and ease of learning Neo4j for SQL developers. We also went through the various licensing and step-by-step installation processes of various flavors of Neo4j. Finally, we also executed the CRUD operations using Cypher in the Neo4j shell, REST, and Neo4j browser.

In the next chapter, we will dive deep into the Cypher constructs pattern and pattern matching for querying Neo4j.

2
Querying the Graph with Cypher

We never live in isolation and this hold true with our data, which is nothing more than an interconnection between varied kinds of domains known as graphs.

Graphs are complex and evolving, so, to extract data from these complex graphs, we need an efficient query mechanism that focuses on the domain model and encourages "What to retrieve?" instead of "How to retrieve?".

Neo4j introduces a powerful, declarative, and SQL-inspired graph query language, Cypher.

Cypher is designed to be a humane query language, that leverages the concepts of pattern and pattern matching and allows for expressive, efficient querying and updating of the graph store. Cypher is a relatively simple but very powerful language.

This chapter will provide you with an in-depth understanding of Cypher as a query language for Neo4j database. It will guide you through the anatomy of Cypher, and then will focus on the heart of Cypher: pattern and pattern matching. We will also discuss a real-world example where we will query complex graphs with Cypher.

At the end of this chapter, you will be well versed in the Cypher constructs and will be able to write Cypher queries for extracting data from complex graphs within no time.

This chapter will cover the following points:

- Basic anatomy of a Cypher query
- Pattern and pattern matching
- Working with nodes and relationships

Basic anatomy of a Cypher query

In this section, we will talk about the need for a new query language, such as Cypher. We will then deep-dive into its constructs, syntax, and structure of Cypher queries for retrieving data from the Neo4j database.

Brief details of Cypher

Over the last 25 years, a lot of research has been done on graph query languages and now, with the advent of Web 2.0, which is focused on collaboration and sharing, they have undergone a recent resurgence. It not only introduced the complexities of linked data, such as social networks, but also highlighted the fact that data is not isolated and is all about connections in it.

As a result, there are many languages that evolved over time and a few of them also gained popularity, such as the ones listed next:

- **SPARQL Protocol and RDF Query Language (SPARQL)**: `http://en.wikipedia.org/wiki/SPARQL`

- **Gremlin**: `http://gremlin.tinkerpop.com/`

- **Metaweb query language (MQL)**: `https://developers.google.com/freebase/v1/mql-overview`

There are many more languages, but all these languages are complex and difficult to maintain. Moreover, they also failed to meet one or more primary goals of the query language of the Neo4j database. Considering all aspects, Neo4j introduced a new graph query language, Cypher, for querying the Neo4j database. Cypher meets the standard goals of graph databases, which are as follows:

- Subgraph matching

- Comparing and returning paths

- Aggregations

- Approximate matching and ranking

Cypher also added some more features such as **Declarative**, **SQL Familiarity**, and **ASCII Pattern**, which led it to be better than all the other graph query languages.

Cypher is a declarative graph query language, which focuses on "What to retrieve" and not "How to retrieve". It is suitable for both developers and operation professionals as it is designed to be a "humane" query language, where its constructs are nothing more than plain-English, which is simple and easy to understand.

It borrows most of its structure from SQL and that's the reason it is also called **SQL alike**. Being close to SQL, SQL developers can easily adapt to the constructs of Cypher.

Inspired by a number of different languages such as SQL, SPARQL, Haskell, and Python, Cypher provides expressive and efficient querying and updating of the graph database.

Let's move ahead and understand the execution phases and basic structure of the Cypher queries.

Cypher execution phases

As we discussed earlier in this chapter, Cypher is designed to be a humane query language, which makes it easy to understand, and it also provides a convenient way to express queries. Execution of a Cypher query is a step-by-step process and there are various phases before the query is finally executed on the graph.

The various phases of the Cypher query execution are listed as follows:

- Parsing, validating, and generating the execution plan
- Locating the initial node(s)
- Selecting and traversing the relationships
- Changing and/or returning the values

Let's briefly understand the activities performed in each of the phases.

Parsing, validating, and generating the execution plan

Parsing and validating Cypher statement(s) is same as we do in the other databases. Though it is important, it is a more or a less standard activity for any language. The critical step is devising or generating the optimal strategy for searching the graph and returning the results to the user in the shortest possible time. Cypher generates the execution plan, which details out the complete strategy for graph traversing and searching the provided nodes in the given graph. This is a bit tricky, and sometimes requires the attention of the developers for analyzing and rewriting their queries for performance optimizations. We will talk about Cypher optimization in detail in *Chapter 3, Mutating Graph with Cypher*.

Locating the initial node(s)

The Cypher queries require a starting point or a node in the graph as the starting point for traversals. Neo4j is capable of traversing billions of nodes in a few seconds and is also highly optimized for traversing property graphs, but searching the complete graph every time is not a good idea. The Cypher queries introduced a schema in Neo4j 2.0+ that provides the facility to define indexes on labels and properties, and these indexes are automatically updated and used by the Cypher queries to find the starting points.

Selecting and traversing the relationships

Neo4j can traverse portions of the graph and perform any requested actions as soon as the initial nodes are determined. The execution plan helps Neo4j to determine the nodes and the relationships that are needed for completing the execution of the Cypher query.

Changing and/or returning the values

This is the final action, once Neo4j has reached the intended node or relationship that was requested by the user. Finally, it commits the modifications/creation/deletion or simply returns the values.

The structure of Cypher

Cypher borrows most of its structure from SQL, which also means that its queries are built up by joining various clauses. A Cypher query is comprised of four major components—nodes, properties, label, and relationships. No matter what you query, all your Cypher queries will use either all or a combination of these components. We briefly talked about the similarity of the Cypher queries with SQL and its components in *Chapter 1*, *Your First Query with Neo4j*; let's now see the various constructs of Cypher and their usage.

Every database has four basic operations—**create**, **read**, **update**, and **delete**, popularly known as the **CRUD** operations. Cypher supports all four operations, but, in comparison, it is more optimized for read operations. This does not mean that you should not perform all the other operations, but the objective behind this is that, no matter what you do, you have to perform the read operation.

Confusing? But don't worry, stay with me and gradually you will be able to understand as we move forward. By the end of this subsection, I assure you that you will agree with me.

Let's move forward and understand the constructs for all these basic operations.

The read operations

Read operations are also known as search operations where you provide a starting point in a graph and the criteria that need to be met to complete the search.

The next sections will explain the constructs used for the read operations:

MATCH

The MATCH construct is one of the most important and primary clauses of Cypher. It is used to specify the patterns that need to be searched in a graph. MATCH is similar to SQL FROM, where we need to specify the appearance of a specific pattern that needs to be searched or scanned to determine the dataset (also known as subgraph) on which further operations need to be performed. MATCH can be used in conjunction with any of the create, update, or delete clauses. It is mostly used in conjunction with the WHERE clause, which specifies and imposes conditions, restrictions, or predicates to the MATCH clause.

Let's take an example of a MATCH statement:

```
MATCH (x:MALE) WHERE x.age is NOT NULL and x.name is NOT NULL RETURN
x;
```

In the preceding example, we are searching the occurrence of all nodes that are labeled with MALE and have the two properties, age and name. Both of them contain some value, and in the end we want them to be returned back to the invoking program, which in our case is a console.

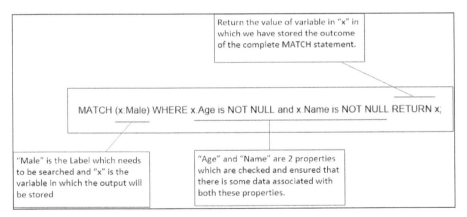

The preceding figure defines the structure of a MATCH statement, where MATCH is always the first clause, and then optionally, it can be preceded by a WHERE clause. At the end, it should return some value. RETURN is the final clause where it signifies the end of the Cypher query. Except in the create clause, all other clauses in the Cypher queries should end with a RETURN clause; otherwise, it is treated as invalid.

Cypher is declarative, and so the query itself does not specify the algorithm for performing the search. Cypher will automatically work out the best approach to find the start nodes and match the patterns.

For example, predicates in the WHERE clauses can be evaluated before pattern matching, during pattern matching, or after finding the matches. However, there are cases where you can influence the decisions taken by the query compiler by specifying the indexes. We will talk about indexes and other Cypher optimizations in *Chapter 3, Mutating Graph with Cypher*.

OPTIONAL MATCH

The OPTIONAL MATCH statement is exactly the same as the MATCH statement, the only difference being that it returns the NULL values for the missing parts of the pattern. It can be considered equivalent to the OUTER JOIN keyword in SQL. If there is no match for the given Cypher query, MATCH does not return any value, not even NULL. However, OPTIONALMATCH returns NULL. For example, the Cypher query given in the previous example can be rewritten as follows:

```
OPTIONAL MATCH (x:MALE) WHERE x.age is NOT NULL and x.name is NULL
RETURN x;
```

The result of the preceding Cypher query would return NULL if no match is found.

START

Every Cypher query can have multiple starting points. Using START, we can introduce the starting points by legacy index lookups. Legacy indexes were used till Neo4j 1.9, but after that they have been replaced with the schema. Legacy indexes are still supported but more towards providing backward-compatibility with the earlier versions of Neo4j. From Neo4j 2.0+, it is recommended you use only the schema, which is implicitly used by the Cypher query during execution. (We will talk in detail about the schema in the next chapter.)

An example of the START query is shown as follows:

```
START n = node:nodesIndx (Name ="John") return n;
```

In the preceding example, we are searching the nodes with the attribute `Name`, and value `"John"`, in the index named as `nodes`.

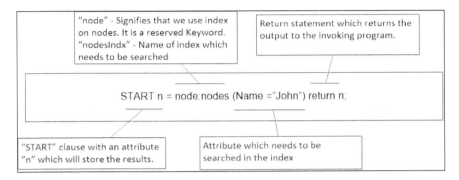

The preceding diagram explains the various adjoining parts of `START` and the process of using `START` in the Cypher queries.

AGGREGATION

Another important concept in Cypher is to perform aggregations on the output of the Cypher queries using various grouping functions such as `count`, `max`, and `min`. Cypher supports a wide variety of grouping functions, starting from the simple `count` function and ranging to statistical functions such as **standard deviation** (`stdev` or `stdevp`), along with functions such as `DISTINCT`.

Let's continue the same example that we used in `MATCH` and `OPTIONAL MATCH`, and return the count of nodes that matches the given criteria:

```
MATCH (x:MALE) WHERE x.age is NOT NULL and x.name is NOT NULL RETURN
count(x);
```

Everything remains the same, except that we replaced x with `count(x)`, which now returns the count of nodes, instead of nodes. Let's consider another scenario where we want to count the number of nodes with a unique name:

```
MATCH (x:MALE) WHERE x.age is NOT NULL and x.name is NOT NULL RETURN
count(DISTINCT x.name);
```

In the preceding statement, everything remains the same, except that we have replaced `count(x)` with `count(DISTINCT x.Name)`, where `DISTINCT` gives us the nodes with a unique name.

 Refer to `http://neo4j.com/docs/stable/query-aggregation.html` for a complete list of aggregation functions.

The create or update operations

The **create** or **update** operations perform the same function as in RDBMS. They create the various graph elements—nodes, properties, labels, and relationships.

Here we will briefly touch upon create and update operations and cover additional details in the next chapter.

The next sections will explain the constructs used to create or update the elements of a graph.

Create

The CREATE operation is used for creating a node, property, or a relationship. It is the only element that does not need to return anything at the end of the statement.

Consider the following example:

```
CREATE (n:MALE {Name: "John", Age: 24});
```

The preceding statement creates a node with the label MALE and two properties, where the Name property is of type string and the Age property is of type integer.

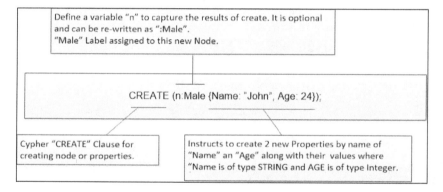

The preceding illustration describes the various parts of the CREATE statement and the way the Cypher query engine interprets the instructions.

 Refer to http://neo4j.com/docs/stable/graphdb-neo4j-properties.html for a complete list of the data types supported by properties in Cypher.

SET

The SET operation is used for updating labels or properties on nodes and relationships.

For example, let's assume that in the preceding query, we need to update the value of Age and change it to 25:

```
match (n:MALE {name:"John"}) SET n.age = 25 return n;
```

The preceding query first searches the records that require modifications, and then uses SET to update the value of the properties.

MERGE

The MERGE operation is a special type of operation that ensures a node, property, label, or relationship exists either by creating a new one or do nothing if it already exists in a given graph. It ensures uniqueness among the nodes and avoids creating any duplicate graph elements. MERGE is accompanied further with two more clauses — ON MATCH and ON CREATE. The ON MATCH clause is executed whenever a match is successful, and ON CREATE is executed whenever a match is not successful and a new element is to be created in the given graph.

Let's see a couple of examples:

```
MERGE (n:MALE {name: "John"}) return n;
```

The preceding example shows a simple MERGE statement that will check whether the given criterion exists. If the given criterion exists, it will not do anything; otherwise, it will create a new node.

```
MERGE (n:MALE {name: "John", age:24})
ON MATCH SET n.age= 25, n.last_updatedtimestamp = timestamp()
ON CREATE SET n.craeted_timestamp = timestamp()
```

The preceding example first matches the criteria provided in the MERGE statement, and then defines two more clauses — ON MATCH and ON CREATE.

ON MATCH will be executed in the scenarios where conditions defined with the MERGE statement are satisfied; otherwise, ON CREATE will be executed. However, in any case, either ON MATCH or ON CREATE will be executed. This would also avoid the creation of duplicate elements.

Downloading the example code

You can download the example code files from your account at http://www.packtpub.com for all the Packt Publishing books you have purchased. If you purchased this book elsewhere, you can visit http://www.packtpub.com/support and register to have the files e-mailed directly to you.

The delete operation

The `delete` operation is used to remove the nodes and relationships from a given graph.

Consider the following example:

```
MATCH (n:MALE {name: "John", age:24}) delete n;
```

In the preceding statement, first we search the node, capture it into a variable n, and then delete it.

The `remove` operation, as shown in the next example, is also used for deleting the properties and labels from the graph.

Consider the following example:

```
MATCH (n:MALE {name: "Andrew", age:24}) remove n.age return n;
```

In the preceding statement, first we search the node, capture it into the variable n, use `remove` to delete one of its properties, namely Age, and then finally return the output.

So, by now you should have understood the reason for optimizing reads in Cypher: because irrespective of any operation (create, update, or delete), we have to first execute the MATCH (read) statement, search for the appropriate location or node in the graph, and only then execute the create, update, or delete statement.

Pattern and pattern matching

Pattern and pattern matching are the heart of Cypher. They describe the shape of the data that we want to search, create, or update within the provided graph. It is imperative to understand pattern and pattern matching as a concept with reference to Cypher, so that you can write effective and efficient queries. Before moving forward, let's create a small dataset, and then let's see how patterns are applied or constructed for various elements of graphs.

Sample dataset

In this section, we will create a small dataset for a social network, which will help us in understanding and executing various examples provided further in this section.

Perform the following steps to create a sample dataset:

1. Open your console or shell and then start your Neo4j server by executing `<$NEO4J_HOME>/bin/neo4j` on the console.

2. On the same console, execute `<$NEO4J_HOME>/bin/neo4j-shell`.

3. Now, execute the following set of statements to clean up your database:

```
MATCH (n)-[r]-(n1) delete n,r,n1;
MATCH (n) delete n;
```

The first query search removes all nodes and their associated relationships, and the second query removes all nodes that do not have any relationships.

4. Next, execute the following set of statements on your Neo4j console to create some entries for males and females:

```
CREATE (bradley:MALE:TEACHER {name:'Bradley', surname:'Green',
age:24, country:'US'});
CREATE (matthew:MALE:STUDENT {name:'Matthew', surname:'Cooper',
age:36, country:'US'});
CREATE (lisa:FEMALE {name:'Lisa', surname:'Adams', age:15,
country:'Canada'});
CREATE (john:MALE {name:'John', surname:'Goodman', age:24,
country:'Mexico'});
CREATE (annie:FEMALE {name:'Annie', surname:'Behr', age:25,
country:'Canada'});
CREATE (ripley:MALE {name:'Ripley', surname:'Aniston',
country:'US'});
```

5. Now execute the following set of statements on your Neo4j console to create relationships between males and females:

```
MATCH(bradley:MALE{name:"Bradley"}),(matthew:MALE{name:"Matthew"})
WITH bradley, matthew
CREATE (bradley)-[:FRIEND]->(matthew) , (bradley)-[:TEACHES]-
>(matthew);
MATCH (bradley:MALE{name:"Bradley"}),(matthew:MALE{name:"Matth
ew"})
WITH bradley,matthew
CREATE (matthew)-[:FRIEND]->(bradley);
MATCH (bradley:MALE{name:"Bradley"}),(lisa:FEMALE{name:"Lisa"})
WITH bradley,lisa
CREATE (bradley)-[:FRIEND]->(lisa);
MATCH (lisa:FEMALE{name:"Lisa"}),(john:MALE{name:"John"})
WITH lisa,john
CREATE (lisa)-[:FRIEND]->(john);
```

```
MATCH (annie:FEMALE{name:"Annie"}),(ripley:MALE{name:"Ripley"})
WITH annie,ripley
CREATE (annie)-[:FRIEND]->(ripley);
MATCH (ripley:MALE{name:"Ripley"}),(lisa:FEMALE{name:"Lisa"})
WITH ripley,lisa
CREATE (ripley)-[:FRIEND]->(lisa);
```

And we are done!

In the next sections, we will explore the various aspects of patterns and pattern matching, and you can execute all the provided examples in this section on the Neo4j console against the sample dataset.

Pattern for nodes

The most basic form of pattern is where we define it by using a pair of parentheses and providing a name within the parentheses. Consider the following example:

```
MATCH (a) return a;or MATCH a return a;
```

In the preceding example, we are describing a pattern for node, and by using MATCH we are requesting to return all the nodes. We can also omit parentheses in case we are not using any properties or labels with nodes. However generally, it is a good practice and it's recommended to use parentheses.

Pattern for labels

Labels are a new addition by Neo4j to standard property graphs. It is something similar to annotating your nodes for grouping or categorizing them into buckets, which further helps in searching. One or more labels can be defined on nodes. Consider the following example:

```
MATCH (n:MALE) return n;or MATCH (n:MALE:TEACHER) return n;
```

In the preceding example, we are searching for all those nodes that are annotated with the label MALE, or with multiple labels, MALE and TEACHER.

Pattern for relationships

Relationships are the connection between two given nodes. They can be unidirectional or bidirectional between the two nodes. They are defined within square brackets and are given a user-defined name for further reference within the search queries.

Unidirectional relationships are specified using an arrow sign with a pointed head specifying the direction in which it is flowing. Consider the following example:

```
MATCH (x:TEACHER)-[r:TEACHES]->(y:STUDENT) return x,r,y;
```

The preceding statement searches for all those nodes that are annotated with the labels TEACHER and STUDENT, and are further linked with the relationship TEACHES. Simply reading or interpreting the preceding statement in plain English will result in — "Give me all the nodes where node x is a teacher and teaches a student; that is, node y". That's the reason we said that Cypher is designed to be a "humane" query language, that can be interpreted just by reading.

Bidirectional relationships are specified using an arrow sign with no pointed head. As the name suggests, it is bidirectional and can flow from either end. Consider the following example:

```
MATCH (x:MALE)-[r:FRIEND]-(y:FEMALE) return x,r,y;
```

The preceding statement searches for all those nodes that are annotated with the labels MALE and FEMALE, and irrespective of any direction, they are related to each other by a relationship named as FRIEND. Simply reading or interpreting the preceding statement in plain English will result in — "Give me all those nodes where node x is a male and node y is a female, and both of them are friends".

Pattern for properties

Properties are the other features of property graphs. One or more properties can be defined for a node or relationship.

Properties are key/value pair wrapped around the curly braces and two properties are separated by a comma. Consider the following example:

```
Match (a:MALE { name: "John", age : 24 }) return a;
```

In the preceding example, we are searching for a node that is annotated with the label MALE and has two properties name and age, with the values as "John" and 24.

Using the where clause with patterns

Pattern alone cannot satisfy all our needs, and that's the reason the where clause was introduced; it can be used with patterns for further filtering of data. The where clause in itself is not a clause and cannot be used independently, but it has to be used in conjunction with MATCH, OPTIONALMATCH, START, or WITH.

Consider the following example:

```
MATCH (n)
where n.name = "John" and n.age< 25
return n;
```

In the preceding example, we are trying to search for those nodes where the value of the name property is "John" and the value of the age property is less than 25.

Let's see some more examples based on the various features provided by where.

Using patterns in the where clause

Patterns are also known as expressions in Cypher and they return collection of paths. The collection expressions are also predicates—an empty collection represents false and a non-empty collection represents true.

We cannot use commas between multiple paths, as we do in MATCH, but we can use AND to specify and combine multiple patterns in a single path.

Consider the following example:

```
MATCH (n)
where n.name IN["John","Andrew"] and n.age is Not Null
return n;
```

In the preceding query, we are using a collection of values for filtering the value of the name property and also instructing it to return only those nodes that have some value of the age property. We can also use Not or regular expressions in the filters.

Consider the following example:

```
MATCH (n)
where n.name =~"J.*"
return n;
```

The preceding query will return all those nodes where the value of the name property starts with the letter J.

Using general clauses with patterns

There are a few other general clauses that can also be used with patterns to make the results more meaningful. Let's discuss these general clauses.

The order by clause

Similar to SQL, Cypher also provides the **order by** clause, which can return the results in a specific order (ascending or descending). Consider the following example:

```
MATCH (n) return n ORDER by n.name, n.age;
```

The preceding query will return the nodes sorted in the ascending order, first by name, and then by the age property of the node. Adding desc at the end of the statement will return the results in descending order.

The limit and skip clauses

The limit clause only returns the subset of the results starting from the top, whereas skip will ignore the given number of elements from the top. Consider the following example:

```
MATCH (n) return n ORDER by n.name, n.age LIMIT 3;
```

The preceding query will only return the first three nodes and ignore the rest of the results/nodes. The following query will only ignore the first three nodes and return the rest of the results/nodes:

```
MATCH (n) return n ORDER by n.name, n.age SKIP 3;
```

We can also use the combination of SKIP and LIMIT to return the results appearing in the middle. Consider the following example:

```
MATCH (n) return n ORDER by n.name, n.age SKIP 3 LIMIT 2;
```

The preceding query will first ignore the first three nodes, return the next two nodes, and ignore the rest of the results/nodes.

The WITH clause

The WITH clause is another important clause where you can join multiple patterns and the outcome of one pattern can be used as an input to the other pattern in single Cypher query. There are multiple usages of WITH, where you can specify single query for reading and writing or limiting the number of nodes passed on the subsequent MATCH clauses, or introduce aggregates, which can be further used in the WHERE clauses. Let's see a few examples:

```
MATCH (x{ name: "Bradley" })--(y)-->()
WITH y, count(*) AS cnt
WHERE cnt> 1
RETURN y;
```

Executing the preceding statement on the Neo4j console will produce results similar to the one shown in the following illustration:

```
neo4j-sh (?)$ MATCH (x { name: "Bradley" })--(y)-->()
> WITH y, count(*) AS cnt
> WHERE cnt > 1
> RETURN y;
+-----------------------------------------------------------------+
| y                                                               |
+-----------------------------------------------------------------+
| Node[15]{name:"Matthew",surname:"Cooper",age:36,country:"US"}   |
+-----------------------------------------------------------------+
1 row
1012 ms
neo4j-sh (?)$
neo4j-sh (?)$
```

The preceding screenshot shows the usage of the WITH clause with the MATCH statement.

The preceding query first provides all the nodes that are connected to the x node (having the name property "Bradley") with an outgoing relationship. It then introduces the aggregate function count to check that the count of nodes connected to x is greater than 1.

Let's see one more example of using the WITH clause in conjunction with the CREATE clause:

```
MATCH (x { name: "Bradley" })--(y)-->()
WITH x
CREATE (n:Male {name:"Smith", Age:"24"})-[r:FRIEND]->(x)
returnn,r,x;
```

The preceding query first provides all the nodes that are connected to the x node (having the name property "Bradley") with an outgoing relationship. It then creates one more node (with the name property "Smith"), which is connected to the node returned by the MATCH clause.

The UNION and UNION ALL clauses

The UNION and UNION ALL clauses work in the same way they work in SQL. While the former joins two MATCH clauses and produces the results without any duplicates, the latter does the same, except it returns the complete dataset and does not remove any duplicates. Consider the following example:

```
MATCH (x:MALE)-[:FRIEND]->() return x.name, labels(x)
UNION
MATCH (x:FEMALE)-[:FRIEND]->()return x.name, labels(x);
```

Executing the preceding query will produce the following results:

```
neo4j-sh (?)$ MATCH (x:MALE)-[:FRIEND]->() return x.name, labels(x)
> UNION
> MATCH (x:FEMALE)-[:FRIEND]->() return x.name, labels(x);
+----------------------------------------------+
| x.name    | labels(x)                        |
+----------------------------------------------+
| "Bradley" | ["MALE","TEACHER"]               |
| "Matthew" | ["MALE","STUDENT"]               |
| "Ripley"  | ["MALE"]                         |
| "Lisa"    | ["FEMALE"]                       |
| "Annie"   | ["FEMALE"]                       |
+----------------------------------------------+
5 rows
719 ms
neo4j-sh (?)$
```

In the preceding query, we are searching all the nodes that have label as either MALE or FEMALE, and are connected with the other nodes with the relationship named as FRIEND. If we replace it with UNION ALL, it will return the complete dataset, which will also have duplicate nodes.

In this section, we discussed the patterns for nodes, labels, relationships, and properties. We also talked about various clauses such as WHERE, UNION, UNION ALL, order by, and WITH, which are used to create and define various patterns for querying the underlying graph database.

Let's work more with nodes and relationships and see some real-world examples in the next section.

Working with nodes and relationships

In this section, we will discuss complex and real world scenarios/problem statements and solve those problem statements with the help of Cypher using pattern and pattern matching.

Let's enhance our sample dataset that we created in the previous section and add some more data. We will add some movies and also have our users provide ratings for them.

Perform the following steps for adding movies and ratings:

1. Open your console or Shell and start your Neo4j server by executing <$NEO4J_HOME>/bin/neo4j on console (in case it is not started).

2. On same console execute <$NEO4J_HOME>/bin/neo4j-shell.

3. Now execute the following set of statements to create some movies:

```
CREATE (firstBlood:MOVIE {name:"First Blood"});
CREATE (avengers:MOVIE {name:"Avengers"});
CREATE (matrix:MOVIE {name:"Matrix"});
```

4. Next, execute the following set of statements on your Neo4j-console to have users rate the movies:

```
MATCH
(bradley:MALE{name:"Bradley"}),(matthew:MALE{name:"Matthew"}),(lis
a:FEMALE{name:"Lisa"}), (john:MALE{name:"John"}), (annie:FEMALE{na
me:"Annie"}),(ripley:MALE{name:"Ripley"}),
(firstBlood:MOVIE {name:"First Blood"}), (avengers:MOVIE
{name:"Avengers"}), (matrix:MOVIE {name:"Matrix"})
WITH bradley, matthew, lisa, john, annie, ripley, firstBlood,
avengers, matrix
CREATE (bradley)-[:HAS_RATED{ratings:5}]->(firstBlood),
  (matthew)-[:HAS_RATED{ratings:4}]->(firstBlood),
  (john)-[:HAS_RATED{ratings:4}]->(firstBlood),
  (annie)-[:HAS_RATED{ratings:4}]->(firstBlood),
  (ripley)-[:HAS_RATED{ratings:4}]->(firstBlood),
  (lisa)-[:HAS_RATED{ratings:5}]->(avengers),
  (matthew)-[:HAS_RATED{ratings:4}]->(avengers),
(annie)-[:HAS_RATED{ratings:3}]->(avengers);
```

And we are done !!!

The final dataset will contain the following features:

We have a few males and females and these males and females are either friends or teacher and student. These males and females also watch movies and provide ratings for those movies.

Now let's analyze the dataset in the form of questions and answers, where we will raise different questions and build/design the Cypher queries to answer those questions. This is also known as uncovering the pattern within the data, which otherwise is difficult to see with the naked eye.

1. I am Bradley and I live in US. Who are the users that live in the same country as I do?

```
Cypher Query - match (x {country:"US"}) return x;
```

The above query searches the country attribute of the users and returns all the users who live in same country as Bradley.

2. How many males have females as friends?

Cypher Query - match (x:MALE)-[r:FRIEND]->(y:FEMALE) return x.name as MaleName,type(r) as Relation,y.name as FemaleName;

Executing the above query on the Neo4j-console will produce the following results:

```
neo4j-sh (?)$ match (x:MALE)-[r:FRIEND]->(y:FEMALE) return x.name as MaleName,ty
pe(r) as Relation,y.name as FemaleName;
+-----------------------------------------+
| MaleName  | Relation | FemaleName |
+-----------------------------------------+
| "Matthew" | "FRIEND" | "Lisa"     |
| "Ripley"  | "FRIEND" | "Lisa"     |
| "Bradley" | "FRIEND" | "Lisa"     |
+-----------------------------------------+
3 rows
109 ms
neo4j-sh (?)$ _
```

The preceding query searches for all males who have females as friends. There are two things which we should focus on in this query. First, that the relationship is uni-directional; that is we are only checking males who are friends with females and not vice-versa, because that was the question. Second, that the as keyword in the RETURN clause, where we are renaming the default column name, is exactly similar to the feature provided by SQL.

3. I am Bradley and I want to know the people who are friends of my friends and are also my friends:

Cypher Query - match (x{name:"Bradley"})-[:FRIEND]->(friend)<-[:FRIEND]-(otherFriend) return distinct friend.name as CommonFriend;

Executing the above query on the Neo4j-console will produce the following results:

```
neo4j-sh (?)$ match (x{name:"Bradley"})-[:FRIEND]->(friend)<-[:FRIEND]-(otherFri
end) return distinct friend.name as CommonFriend;
+--------------+
| CommonFriend |
+--------------+
| "Lisa"       |
+--------------+
1 row
125 ms
neo4j-sh (?)$ _
```

The preceding query searches for all the friends of Bradley and then further queries their friends using the MATCH statement.

4. I am Bradley and I want to know the people who are friends of my friends but are not my friends:

```
Cypher Query - Match (me{name:"Bradley"})-[r:FRIEND]-
(myFriend),(myFriend)-[:FRIEND]-(otherFriend)
where NOT (me)-[:FRIEND]-(otherFriend)
return otherFriend.name as NotMyFriends;
```

Executing the above query on the Neo4j-console will produce the following results:

```
neo4j-sh (?)$ Match (me{name:"Bradley"})-[r:FRIEND]-(myFriend),(myFriend)-[:FRIE
ND]-(otherFriend)
> where NOT (me)-[:FRIEND]-(otherFriend)
> return otherFriend.name as NotMyFriends;
+--------------------+
! NotMyFriends !
+--------------------+
! "John" !
! "Ripley" !
+--------------------+
2 rows
163 ms
neo4j-sh (?)$
```

The preceding query searches for all the friends of `Bradley` and then further queries their friends using the MATCH statement. The relationship is bi-directional because now we do not care and we need to find all the nodes which are not connected to `Bradley` but are connected to each FRIEND of `Bradley`.

5. Find out all the movies and the number of times they have been rated by the users:

```
Cypher Query - MATCH (movie:MOVIE)<-[r:HAS_RATED*0..]-
(person)
return  movie.name as Movie, count(person)-1 as
countOfRatings order by countOfRatings;
```

Executing the above query on the Neo4j-console will produce the following results:

```
neo4j-sh (?)$ MATCH (person)-[r:HAS_RATED*0..]->(movie:MOVIE)
> return  movie.name as Movie, count(person)-1 as countOfRatings order by countO
fRatings;
+---------------------------------------+
! Movie       ! countOfRatings !
+---------------------------------------+
! "Matrix"    ! 0 !
! "Avengers"  ! 3 !
! "First Blood" ! 5 !
+---------------------------------------+
3 rows
156 ms
neo4j-sh (?)$
```

The preceding query searches for all the movies and then searches for persons who have rated them. When we use 0 in variable length paths then two identifiers can point to the same node. If the distance between two nodes is zero, they are by definition the same node. So to avoid the count of same nodes, we are simply doing -1 from the total count that provides us with the exact count of ratings for all movies in our database.

6. Find out all the movies that are rated by Bradley and have also been rated by his friends:

```
Cypher Query - match (x{name:"Bradley"})-[:FRIEND]-
>(friend)-[r:HAS_RATED]->(movie) return friend.name as
Person, r.ratings as Ratings,movie.name as Movie;
```

Executing the above query on the Neo4j-console will produce the following results:

```
neo4j-sh (?)$ match (x{name:"Bradley"})-[:FRIEND]->(friend)-[r:HAS_RATED]->(movi
e) return friend.name as Person, r.ratings as Ratings,movie.name as Movie;
+-----------------------------------------------+
| Person    | Ratings | Movie          |
+-----------------------------------------------+
| "Lisa"    | 5       | "Avengers"     |
| "Matthew" | 4       | "First Blood"  |
| "Matthew" | 4       | "Avengers"     |
+-----------------------------------------------+
3 rows
203 ms
neo4j-sh (?)$ _
```

The preceding query first searches for all the friends of Bradley and then filters out all friends of Bradley who have rated the movies. Finally, it returns the results along with the rating of different movies provided by Bradley's friends.

In this section, we discussed various kinds of real-world examples, learned how to understand the questions, and discussed the strategy that should be used for building/creating/designing Cypher queries.

Summary

In this chapter we have learned about the similarity and ease of learning Neo4j for SQL developers, we have gone through licensing and the step-by-step installation process of various flavors of Neo4j and finally we have also executed CRUD operations using Cypher in Neo4jshell, ReST, and Neo4j Browser.

In next chapter, we will deep-dive into the Cypher constructs and Pattern and Pattern matching, for querying Neo4j.

3
Mutating Graph with Cypher

Writing to databases or mutating the underlying data in databases' is one of the important aspects of any **Database Management System (DBMS)**. It provides a structure to your data within the underlying datastore. It is imperative to have a performance-efficient mechanism for mutation, so that your graph database can be available for further querying in the shortest possible time.

Apart from being performance-efficient, we also need to ensure that the mutation/ write process follows the following principles of transaction management:

- **Atomicity (all or nothing)**: Every write is atomic in nature, so that if any part of a transaction fails, the database state is left unchanged

- **Consistency (from one valid state to another)**: At any point in time, data in the database is in a consistent state where all users read the same data

- **Isolation**: Each transaction should occur independently and modified data should not be accessible to any other operations during a transaction

- **Durability**: Completed transactions should remain persistent

These four principles are popularly known as ACID properties.

Neo4j has all the features of a DBMS where it is not only performance-efficient but also transactional, supports ACID properties, and finally ensures data integrity, resulting in a good transaction behavior.

In the last chapter, we discussed the read aspects of Neo4j. In this chapter, we will talk and discuss the write aspects of Neo4j.

This chapter will cover the following topics:

- Creating nodes and relationships
- Transforming nodes and relationships
- Cypher query optimizations

Creating nodes and relationships

In this section, we will discuss the various syntactical details for creating nodes and relationships using Cypher.

Nodes and relationships are the two most important elements of Neo4j graph databases. They are created using the CREATE clause of Cypher. Let us move forward and understand the process of creating nodes and relationships using Cypher.

Working with nodes

Node is one of the core elements of Neo4j database. Every other element of Neo4j is either connected to nodes or is used to enhance the definition/description of a node. Let us delete the existing data, which we created in the previous chapter from our Neo4j database, and then see the step-by-step process of creating nodes.

Perform the following steps to clean up your Neo4j database:

1. Open your Linux console or shell and execute `<$NEO4J_HOME>/bin/neo4j-shell`.

2. Execute the following Cypher queries to delete the data from the Neo4j database:

    ```
    MATCH (n)-[r]-(n1) delete r,n.n1;
    MATCH n delete n;
    ```

3. And we are done !!!

The preceding Cypher queries deleted all nodes and relationships from your Neo4j database. Let us move forward and now see the creation of nodes with the CREATE clause.

Single node

The following is the query for creating a single node:

*   `CREATE (n);` or `CREATE ();` or `CREATE (n) return n;`

The preceding query creates a single node. In the CREATE statement we can define a user-defined variable for unique identification of the node, which can further query or refer to the node within the same scope. For example, we have defined n in the preceding Cypher query but in case we do not plan to use it in the same context anywhere further, we can omit n and just define the empty brackets.

The CREATE statements may or may not be preceded with the return clause. In case we use the return clause then it will return and print the output of the CREATE clause; if we do not use return, then it will silently create the given entities in the CREATE clause and will not return or print anything on the console.

Neo4j assigns a unique ID to each and every node, which uniquely identifies and distinguishes each and every node within the Neo4j database. These unique IDs are internal to Neo4j and may vary with each and every Neo4j installation or version. It is advisable not to build any user-defined logic using these node IDs.

The output of the previous Cypher query will produce the following result:

```
neo4j-sh (?)$ CREATE (n) return n;
+--------------------+
! n                  !
+--------------------+
! Node[42]()         !
+--------------------+
1 row
Nodes created: 1
78 ms
neo4j-sh (?)$
```

The preceding illustration shows the output of the CREATE clause. As we have used the return clause, so the output of the CREATE clause is printed on the console. Node IDs are defined in square brackets, in our case [42]. Though it is not advisable/recommended to develop any user-defined logic around the node IDs but if in the rarest of rare cases you still want to, then you can use ID(<Ref of Node>) for querying upon the node IDs. For example, to print all node IDs within our Neo4j database, we can execute the following Cypher statement:

```
MATCH (n) return ID(n);
```

You can use the ID() function with other clauses such as where. For example, you can execute the following Cypher statement to search a particular node using the node ID:

```
MATCH (n) where id(n)=42 return n;
```

```
neo4j-sh (?)$ match (n) where id(n)=42 return n;
+--------------------+
! n                  !
+--------------------+
! Node[42]()         !
+--------------------+
1 row
127 ms
```

The previous illustration shows the output of the query using ID() in the where clause. However, as we earlier discussed, node IDs are internal to Neo4j, so the output of the preceding statement may vary and will depend upon the installation and versions of the Neo4j database.

Multiple nodes

The CREATE statement allows us to create multiple nodes in a single CREATE clause. For example:

- CREATE (n), (n1); or CREATE (), (); or CREATE (n), (n1) return n, n1;

Everything remains the same as we did for creating a single node, except that the preceding Cypher statement adds a comma and defines some more nodes to create multiple nodes using the CREATE clause. The outcome of the preceding statement may vary and will depend upon the installation and versions of Neo4j Database.

Node with labels

Neo4j provides the feature of tagging/grouping/categorizing similar nodes by associating them with a label. Labels can be further used to create an index and also help in optimized searching of nodes. The following is the Cypher query that creates a node with a label:

- CREATE (:MALE); or CREATE (n:MALE) return n;

Executing the preceding statement on Neo4j-shell will produce results that will be similar to the following illustration:

```
neo4j-sh (?)$ CREATE (n:MALE) return n;
+-----------+
! n         !
+-----------+
! Node[0]{} !
+-----------+
1 row
Nodes created: 1
Labels added: 1
4329 ms
neo4j-sh (?)$
```

In the previous statement, we are creating a node that is tagged with a label named as MALE. On Neo4j-shell, we can see the results as shown in the preceding illustration — **Nodes Created: 1** and **Labels added: 1**.

Now we can search this newly created node by referencing the label in our search queries. For example, the following is the Cypher query that searches all the nodes associated with the label MALE:

```
MATCH (n:MALE) return n;
```

We can also add or associate a node with more than one label. For example, we can also add the country as another label:

```
MATCH (n:MALE:US) return n;
```

Node with properties

Properties are another important element of Neo4j. Properties are the key-value pairs and we can define and associate them either with nodes or relationship. Properties hold the actual data which can be further used in searching. The following is the Cypher query that creates a node with properties:

```
CREATE (x:MALE{name:"John"});
```

In the preceding query, we are creating a node that is tagged with a label MALE, and at the same time it also contains an attribute name. We can define more than one attribute for a node by separating each of them by a comma. For example, in the previous query we can add the age attribute and the new Cypher query would be as follows:

```
CREATE (x:MALE{name:"John",age:25});
```

Running the preceding query will produce following results:

```
neo4j-sh (?)$ CREATE (x:MALE{name:"John",age:25});
+---------------------+
| No data returned. |
+---------------------+
Nodes created: 1
Properties set: 2
Labels added: 1
1703 ms
neo4j-sh (?)$
```

As shown in the previous screenshot, executing the query we just created will add a node, label, and property in a single Cypher CREATE statement.

Properties also provide flexibility to define the data types. For example, in the previous example we defined two properties—name, which is of type String, and age, which is of type Integer. Property values can either be a primitive or an array of primitive. NULL is not a valid value of a property but can be handled by not defining the key.

The following is a list of data types supported by properties:

Type	Description	Range of Values
Boolean		`true/false`
byte or byte[]	A single byte or array of bytes. It is an 8-byte Integer.	`-128` to `127`, inclusive of both ends.
short or short[]	A single short or array of shorts. It is a 16-byte Integer.	`-32768` to `32767`, inclusive of both ends.
int or int[]	A single integer or array of integers. It is a 32-byte Integer.	`-2147483648` to `2147483647`, inclusive of both ends.
long or long[]	A single long or array of longs. It is a 64-byte Integer.	`-9223372036854775808` to `9223372036854775807`, inclusive of both ends.
float or float[]	32-bit IEEE 754 floating-point number.	
double or double[]	64-bit IEEE 754 floating-point number.	
char or char[]	16-bit unsigned integers representing Unicode characters.	`0` to `65535`
String or String[]	It is a sequence of Unicode characters.	

Let's take an example where we have to define a node with a label `MALE` and property `country_visited`, which is of type String[]. Refer to the following code:

```
CREATE (n:MALE {country_visited:["US","India","China"]});
```

Array of values are defined within the square brackets, same as we have defined in the previous Cypher query. Similarly, we can define the array of other data types within the square brackets. Even while searching, we have to use the same format where we have to define the search criteria for arrays within square brackets:

```
match (n:MALE{country_visited: ["US","India","China"]}) return n;
```

Working with relationships

Relationships are another core element and the heart of Neo4j graphs. There is no significance of any node or property until and unless it is connected to other nodes, which essentially defines the connection between two entities and their relationship with each other. We briefly touched upon the relationships in the previous chapter where we talked about the significance of relationships in pattern and pattern-matching. Let us get down to basics and see the process of creating relationships between two (or more than two) nodes.

To begin with, let's clean up our database and then see the step-by-step process of creating nodes and relationships.

Perform the following steps to clean up your Neo4j database:

1. Open your Linux console or shell and execute `"<$NEO4J_HOME>/bin/neo4j-shell"`.

2. Execute the following Cypher queries to delete the data from Neo4j database:
    ```
    MATCH (n)-[r]-(n1) delete r,n.n1;
    MATCH n delete n;
    ```

3. The preceding Cypher queries deleted all the nodes and relationships from your Neo4j database. Let's move forward and now see the creation of relationships with the CREATE clause.

Single relationships

Relationships can be unidirectional (-> or <-) or bidirectional (-), are defined in square brackets, and are given a user-defined name that can be further referred in the search queries.

The following is a Cypher statement to create a unidirectional relationship between two nodes:

```
CREATE (n:MALE{name:"John"})-[r:FRIEND]->(n:FEMALE {name: "Kate"});
```

or

```
CREATE (n:MALE{name:"John"})-[r:FRIEND]->(n1:FEMALE {name: "Kate"})
return n,r,n1;
```

Executing the preceding Cypher statement will produce the following results:

```
neo4j-sh (?)$ CREATE (n:MALE{name:"John"})-[r:FRIEND]->(n1:FEMALE{name:"Kate"});
+-----------------------+
| No data returned. |
+-----------------------+
Nodes created: 2
Relationships created: 1
Properties set: 2
Labels added: 2
204 ms
neo4j-sh (?)$ _
```

In the previous query, we are creating two nodes, one relationship, and two properties. Let us understand the different parts of the query through the following diagram:

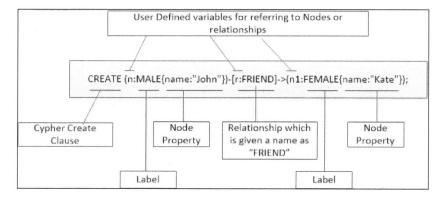

The preceding figure defines the various parts of a Cypher query and how they are connected with each other to create a relationship between two nodes.

Multiple relationships

Multiple relationships are created in the same way as we created a single relationship. The only difference here is that we are creating more than one relationship between more than one node.

For example, let's assume that we need to create four different nodes with the following specifications:

- Node with a label MALE and a property name with a value Pat
- Node with a label MALE and a property name with a value Smith
- Pat and Smith are friends

- Node with a label FEMALE and a property name with a value as Kate
- Smith and Kate are friends
- Node with a label FEMALE and a property name with a value Kim
- Kate and Kim are friends

Complex isn't it? Actually it is not.

If we follow the instructions as they are defined and start forming the Cypher query following each step, then we will see that it is very easy.

Considering the preceding example, the following are the steps for forming the Cypher query:

1. Create a Cypher query to create a node with property name with value Pat:

   ```
   CREATE (m1:MALE{name:"Pat"})
   ```

2. Create a Cypher query to create a node with property name with value Smith:

   ```
   CREATE (m1:MALE{name:"Smith"})
   ```

3. Next, define the relationship between Pat and Smith, and give the name of that relationship as FRIEND:

   ```
   CREATE (m1:MALE{name:"Pat"})-[r1:FRIEND]-> (m2:MALE
   {name:"Smith"})
   ```

4. And so on......

5. The final Query will look as follows:

   ```
   CREATE (m1:MALE{name:"Pat"})-[r1:FRIEND]->
   (m2:MALE{name:"Smith"})-[r2:FRIEND]->(f1:FEMALE{name:"Kate"})-
   [r3:FRIEND]->(f2:FEMALE{name:"Kim"})
   return m1.name, type(r1), m2.name, type(r2), f1.name, type(r3),
   f2.name;
   ```

6. Execute the preceding query on your neo4j-console and the results will be similar to the following screenshot:

```
neo4j-sh (?)$ CREATE (m1:MALE{name:"Pat"})-[r1:FRIEND]-> (m2:MALE{name:"Smith"})
-[r2:FRIEND]->(f1:FEMALE{name:"Kate"})-[r3:FRIEND]->(f2:FEMALE{name:"Kim"})
> return m1.name, type(r1), m2.name, type(r2), f1.name, type(r3), f2.name;
+-----------------------------------------------------------------------------+
| m1.name | type(r1) | m2.name | type(r2) | f1.name | type(r3) | f2.name |
+-----------------------------------------------------------------------------+
| "Pat"   | "FRIEND" | "Smith" | "FRIEND" | "Kate"  | "FRIEND" | "Kim"   |
+-----------------------------------------------------------------------------+
1 row
Nodes created: 4
Relationships created: 3
Properties set: 4
Labels added: 4
203 ms
neo4j-sh (?)$
```

7. The previous illustration shows the creation of multiple relationships within a single CREATE statement. You can open your Neo4j browser by opening URL http://localhost:7474/ and clicking on **Get Some Data** from your navigation pane on the left-hand side of your browser. You will see something similar to the following illustration:

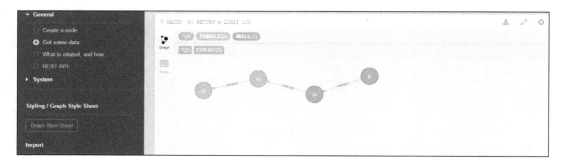

For more information on Neo4j browser, refer to *Chapter 1, Your First Query with Neo4j*.

 The CREATE clause does not provide any syntax for defining bidirectional relationships. However we can execute two CREATE statements with the same set of nodes, but one with à and other withß.

Relationships with properties

Similar to nodes, we can also define properties for relationships. For example, let's assume that we need to create two nodes and connect these nodes with relationship named as MARRIED_TO, and also define a property as year_of_marriage. The Cypher query would be:

```
CREATE (n:MALE{name:"John"})-[r:MARRIED_TO {year_of_marriage:1978}]-
>(f:FEMALE {name: "Kate"}) return n.name, type(r),f.name;
```

The Cypher query we just saw is similar to what we used for nodes, except that here apart from nodes we are also defining the property of the relationship within the curly braces.

Nodes and relationships with full paths

We can also capture the complete CREATE clause and pattern into a variable, so that all parts of the pattern which are not in scope can be created. For example, the previous statement can be rewritten as follows:

```
CREATE p = (n:MALE{name:"John"})-[r:MARRIED_TO
{year_of_marriage:1978}]->(f:FEMALE {name: "Kate"})
return p;
```

Creating unique nodes and relationships

In all the preceding examples, we have seen that the CREATE statement is used to create new nodes, but the only issue is that it blindly creates them and this may cause duplicates if the nodes already exist within the given graph.

In order to avoid any duplicate nodes, Neo4j provides CREATE UNIQUE. The CREATE UNIQUE statement is somewhere in between MATCH and CREATE, where it will match whatever it can and will create the missing elements.

It uses the existing parts of the graphs and ensures the fewest possible changes to the given graph without any duplicates. It will throw an error in case it finds the existence of the same patterns at multiple places in the given graph, and so we need to ensure that the pattern provided in the CREATE UNIQUE statement should be unique.

For example, refer to the following:

```
match (andres { name:'Andres' })
CREATE UNIQUE (andres { name:'Andres' })-[:WORKS_WITH]->(michael {
name:'Michael' });
```

In the preceding example, CREATE UNIQUE will match the given pattern and will then evaluate the remaining pattern. It will see whether any relationship exists between node Andres and node Michael; and if not, then it will create a new relationship and node.

CREATE UNIQUE and MERGE

We discussed the MERGE clause in *Chapter 2, Querying the Graph with Cypher*. Let's have a quick recap and then we will discuss some more examples/capabilities of MERGE.

The MERGE clause is a combination of MATCH and CREATE. It searches for a given node, property, label, or relationship; if it already exists in a given graph, then nothing is done, but if not found, then it creates a new one. Similar to CREATE UNIQUE, it ensures uniqueness among the nodes and avoids creating any duplicate graph elements. The only difference is that CREATE UNIQUE can work on partial matches while MERGE either creates a whole pattern or does nothing at all. It is like all or nothing.

The MERGE clause is accompanied further with two more clauses — ON MATCH and ON CREATE. The ON MATCH clause is executed whenever a match is successful, and ON CREATE is executed whenever a match is not successful and a new element is to be created in the given graph. In contrast to CREATE UNIQUE, MERGE can work upon indexes and labels, and can even be used for single node creation.

Let's take an example and create three nodes and then define the relationship between all the three. Refer to the following query:

```
CREATE (f1:FEMALE {name: "Sheena"}), (m:MALE {name: "Oliver"}),
(f2:FEMALE {name:"Sally"}),
f1-[r:FRIEND]->m-[r1:FRIEND]->f2 return f1.name,r,m.name,r1,f2.name;
```

Next, let's assume that we also need to create a relationship between `Sally` and `Sheena`, but at the same time need to ensure that they both are also connected to `Oliver`.

So here we will use the MERGE statement that will match the existing elements and will create the missing elements:

```
MATCH (f1:FEMALE {name: "Sheena"}), (m:MALE {name: "Oliver"}),
(f2:FEMALE {name:"Sally"})
MERGE f1-[r:FRIEND]->m-[r1:FRIEND]->f2-[r2:FRIEND]->f1 return
f1.name,r,m.name,r1,f2.name;
```

 The MERGE clause was introduced in Neo4j 2.0.x and may replace CREATE UNIQUE.

Working with constraints

Neo4j 2.0.x introduced the concept of applying constraints on labels. As of now, only UNIQUE constraint is available but in future it is expected to have more constraints.

The following is the syntax for creating a UNIQUE constraint on a label MALE:

```
CREATE CONSTRAINT ON (n:MALE) ASSERT n.name IS UNIQUE;
```

This previous statement will create a constraint on label `MALE` and ensure that the property `name` is unique.

For dropping the constraint, you simply need to execute the following statement:

```
DROP CONSTRAINT ON (n:MALE) ASSERT n.name IS UNIQUE;
```

Constraint also helps in the `MERGE` statement where, if it finds the existing nodes, then it simply returns and does not create any duplicate nodes. For example, executing the next statement will simply return as we already `UNIQUE` constraint on the nodes having label as `MALE`:

```
MERGE (f:FEMALE {name: "Sheena"}) return f;
```

Transforming nodes and relationships

In this section, we will discuss updating labels, properties, and relationships.

Updating node properties

The properties of a node are modified by using the following Cypher statement:

```
MATCH (f:FEMALE {name: "Sheena"})
SET f.surname = "Foster"
return f;
```

The preceding statement will find the node `Sheena` and will add or update (if it already exists) the property `surname` with a new or modified value. For removing the property, just replace the `SET` statement in the preceding Cypher query with `SET f.surname = NULL`. We can also set multiple properties by separating them with a comma.

The `REMOVE` statement is another construct provided by Cypher for removing the properties of a node. For example, we can also execute the following statement for removing the property `surname`:

```
MATCH (f:FEMALE {name: "Sheena"})
REMOVE f.surname
return f;
```

Updating a label

Labels can also be updated in the same fashion as node properties. Continuing our previous example, let's add one more labels to our existing node Sheena, which identifies the meal preference — vegetarian or non-vegetarian:

```
MATCH (f:FEMALE {name: "Sheena"})
SET f:NONVEG
return f;
```

Now let's assume Sheena changed her meal preferences and decided to be a vegetarian; so now we need to execute the following statement to modify the label:

```
MATCH (f:FEMALE {name: "Sheena"})
REMOVE f:NONVEG
SET f:VEG
return f;
```

We can also add multiple labels by separating them with a : symbol. For example, let's assume we also need to add the country as a label for the node Sheena, so the previous SET statement can now be rewritten as SET f:VEG:US.

 Setting a label on a node that already has the same label will not make any changes to the node. Setting labels is an idempotent operation.

Updating relationships

Unlike properties and labels, there is no syntax for updating relationships. The only process to update relationships is to first remove them and then create new relationships. For example, let's assume that Sheena and Oliver are not friends any longer, so we will execute the following Cypher statement to remove the relationship FRIEND between them:

```
MATCH (f1:FEMALE {name: "Sheena"})-[r:FRIEND]-(f2:MALE
{name:"Oliver"})
DELETE r;
```

Cypher query optimizations

In this section, we will talk about the various utilities, features, tips, and tricks available and provided by Neo4j to improve the performance of our Cypher queries.

Before moving forward, let's clean up our database once again and recreate our sample dataset.

Perform the following steps to clean up your Neo4j database:

1. Open your Linux console or shell and execute `"<$NEO4J_HOME>/bin/neo4j-shell"`.

2. Execute the following Cypher queries to delete the data from Neo4j database.
    ```
    MATCH (n)-[r]-(n1) delete r,n.n1;
    MATCH n delete n;
    ```

Next, recreate the sample dataset provided in the *Pattern and pattern matching* section of *Chapter 2, Querying the Graph with Cypher*.

Further in this section, we will refer to the data created by our sample dataset and will also explain the process of performance tuning/optimization.

Indexes

Neo4j 2.0 introduces an optional schema, based on the concepts of labels. You can define the constraints and indexes on the labels. This in turn helps in implementing data integrity checks and at the same time also helps in performance optimizations of the Cypher query.

We discussed the constraints in the previous section, *Working with constraints*. Let's move forward and see the usage and benefits of indexes.

Indexes in Neo4j are similar to the indexes defined in RDBMS. They help in improving the performance of node lookups. They are automatically updated with all the modifications done to the underlying data structure. Indexes in Neo4j are eventually available, that means that they are being populated in the background and are automatically used as soon as they are **online** and available to serve user requests. In case something goes wrong then indexes can be in **failed** state and we need to look at the errors and recreate/rebuild them.

Indexes are leveraged automatically by Cypher queries. Cypher provides a Query Planner/Optimizer, which evaluates a given Cypher query and makes all possible attempts to execute it in the shortest possible time by scanning the indexes.

Let's look at the process of creating indexes:

*   The following Cypher statement creates an index on label `MALE` and property `name`:
    ```
    CREATE INDEX ON :MALE(name);
    ```

- For listing the available indexes, execute the following command on your `neo4j-shell`:

  ```
  Schema ls
  ```

- The following Cypher command can be used to delete the indexes:

  ```
  DROP INDEX ON :MALE(name);
  ```

Once indexes are defined, they are automatically used whenever the indexed properties are defined in the WHERE clause of our Cypher queries for simple equality comparison or in conditions. However, there could be scenarios where we want to explicitly use a particular index in our Cypher queries and for that we can use the USING clause in our Cypher queries.

For example, execute the following Cypher query and define an index on label MALE (if not already created):

```
CREATE INDEX ON :MALE(name);
```

Check whether the index is successfully created and is ready to serve the request (it should be online):

```
schema ls
```

Once the index is successfully created, let's execute the next query that leverages the USING clause to explicitly state the index to be used while filtering the nodes:

```
MATCH (n:MALE)
USING INDEX n:MALE(name)
where n.name="Matthew"
return n;
```

```
neo4j-sh (?)$ CREATE INDEX ON :MALE(name);
+----------------------+
! No data returned. !
+----------------------+
Indexes added: 1
32 ms
neo4j-sh (?)$ schema ls
Indexes
  ON :MALE(name) ONLINE

No constraints
neo4j-sh (?)$ MATCH (n:MALE)
> USING INDEX n:MALE(name)
> where n.name="Matthew"
> return n;
+----------------------------------------------------------------------+
! n                                                                    !
+----------------------------------------------------------------------+
! Node[4]{name:"Matthew",surname:"Cooper",age:36,country:"US"} !
+----------------------------------------------------------------------+
1 row
78 ms
neo4j-sh (?)$
```

The preceding screenshot shows the process and output of the explicitly stating indexes in the Cypher query.

We can also specify multiple USING clauses in a single query and provide index hints to Cypher Query Optimizer to use multiple indexes. We can also provide the hint to our Cypher Query Planner to scan all the labels first and then perform any further filtering. This could result in a good performance boost in case your query eliminates unnecessary data using labels itself.

For example, we can rewrite our previous query and provide hints to use SCAN:

```
MATCH (n:MALE)
USING SCAN n:MALE
where n.name="Matthew"
return n;
```

There would be no change in results but it could provide a performance boost in case the labels are carefully applied to the nodes.

Index sampling

The first step in executing any Cypher query is to come up with an efficient execution plan. This execution plan is created by Neo4j but before that it needs information about our database, indexes, number of nodes in indexes, relationships, and so on. All this information will assist Neo4j in coming up with an effective and efficient execution plan, which in turn will result in a faster response time for our queries. We will discuss execution plans in the next section, but one of the ways to help Neo4j in arriving at an effective execution plan is index sampling. Index sampling is the process where we analyze and sample our indexes from time to time, and keep the statistics of our indexes updated; these keep on changing as we add, delete, or modify data in the underlying database.

We can instruct Neo4j to automatically sample our indexes from time to time by enabling the following properties in `<$NEO4J_HOME>/conf/neo4j.properties`:

- `index_background_sampling_enabled`: This is a Boolean property that is by default set to `False`. We need to make it `True` for automatic sampling.
- `index_sampling_update_percentage`: It defines the percentage size of the index which needs to be modified before Neo4j triggers sampling.

We can also manually trigger the sampling from `neo4j-console` by using the `schema` command:

- `schema sample -a`: This will trigger the sampling of all the indexes
- `schema sample -l MALE -p name`: This will trigger the sampling on the index defined on label `MALE` and the property `name`

> Append `-f` to the `schema` command to force the sampling of all or a specific index.

Understanding execution plans

Neo4j implements a **cost based optimizer** (**CBO**) that generates an execution plan for each and every query, and defines the exact process to be followed for producing the results of the provided Cypher query. We can analyze the execution plan by two different ways:

- `EXPLAIN`: If we want to see the execution plan of our Cypher query but do not want to execute it, then we can prefix our queries with the `EXPLAIN` keyword and it will show the execution plan of our Cypher query but will not produce any results
- `PROFILE`: If we want to execute our queries and also see the execution plan of our Cypher query, then we can prefix our queries with the `PROFILE` keyword and it will show the execution plan of our Cypher query along with the results

For example, let's understand the execution plan of the following query, which finds a person by the name `Annie`:

```
PROFILE MATCH(n) where n.name="Annie"
return n;
```

The preceding query will produce the following results:

```
neo4j-sh (?)$ PROFILE MATCH(n) where n.name="Annie"
> return n;
+-----------------------------------------------------------+
| n                                                         |
+-----------------------------------------------------------+
| Node[7]{name:"Annie",surname:"Behr",age:25,country:"Canada"} |
+-----------------------------------------------------------+
1 row
47 ms
Compiler CYPHER 2.2

Planner COST

Filter
  |
  +AllNodesScan

+------------+---------------+------+-------+-------------+----------------------------------------------+
|  Operator  | EstimatedRows | Rows | DbHits| Identifiers |                                        Other |
+------------+---------------+------+-------+-------------+----------------------------------------------+
|     Filter |             1 |    1 |    18 |           n | Property(n,name(0)) == ( AUTOSTRING0)       |
| AllNodesScan|            9 |    9 |    10 |           n |                                              |
+------------+---------------+------+-------+-------------+----------------------------------------------+

Total database accesses: 28
neo4j-sh (?)$ _
```

Wow!!!! Lot of information but believe me it is helpful and easy too.

Let's understand the important aspects of the execution plan shown in the preceding illustration:

- **Compiler CYPHER 2.2**: This tells us the version of the compiler which is used to generate this explain plain.

- **Planner COST**: This tells us that Neo4j is using cost based optimizer and the next set of statements will show the execution plan of our query.

- **Filter**: This is the starting point and it signifies that the provided query will use a filter to produce the results.

- **AllNodesScan**: This is the second step within **Filter** and signifies that Cypher will be scanning all the nodes for generating the results. If you are familiar with Oracle then it is similar to **Full Table Scan** (**FTS**) shown in the explain plain of SQL.

Now let's understand the various columns of the table shown in the preceding screenshot:

- **Operator**: This shows the kind of operators used for the execution of the query. In the screenshot being discussed, it shows two operators—**Filter** and **AllNodesScan**. Depending on the given Cypher query, a different filter will be applied.

- **EstimatedRows**: This defines the estimated number of rows that need to be scanned by a particular filter.

- **Rows**: This defines the number of actual rows scanned by the filter.

- **DbHits**: This is the number of actual hits (or I/O) performed for producing the results by a particular filter.

- **Identifiers**: This refers to the identifiers defined and used for each filter.
- **Other**: It refers to any other information associated with the filters.

Easy, isn't it?

Let's move onto the next section and see how these plans can help us in improving the overall performance of our queries.

Analyzing and optimizing queries

In this section, we will talk about the step-by-step process for analyzing and optimizing Cypher queries with an appropriate example.

Let's continue with our example provided in the previous section, and further analyze and perform optimizations. The query in consideration is as follows:

```
PROFILE MATCH(n) where n.name="Annie"
return n;
```

As we have seen earlier, our query uses **AllNodesScan** which is not at all good to have in production systems. It will result in a very heavy operation where it will scan all the nodes, which means the complete database.

In order to optimize our query, let's first analyze our `where` clause where we are filtering by `name="Annie"`. We know that `Annie` is a female and while creating the dataset we also tagged the node `Annie` with a label `FEMALE`.

So let's see if introducing a label in our query will optimize our query.

The modified query will be as follows:

```
PROFILE MATCH(n:FEMALE) where n.name="Annie"
return n;
```

```
neo4j-sh (?)$ PROFILE MATCH(n:FEMALE) where n.name="Annie"
> return n;
+------------------------------------------------------------+
| n                                                          |
+------------------------------------------------------------+
| Node[7]{name:"Annie",surname:"Behr",age:25,country:"Canada"} |
+------------------------------------------------------------+
1 row
93 ms

Compiler CYPHER 2.2

Planner COST

Filter
  |
  +NodeByLabelScan


+--------------+---------------+------+--------+-------------+----------------------------------------+
|     Operator | EstimatedRows | Rows | DbHits | Identifiers |                                  Other |
+--------------+---------------+------+--------+-------------+----------------------------------------+
|       Filter |             0 |    1 |      4 |           n | Property(n,name(0)) == ( AUTOSTRING0)   |
| NodeByLabelScan |          2 |    2 |      3 |           n |                                 :FEMALE |
+--------------+---------------+------+--------+-------------+----------------------------------------+
Total database accesses: 7
```

The modified query has drastically improved the overall performance and time taken by the Cypher query.

The filters have changed and now it is using `NodeByLabelScan`, which is much better as it is now filtering upon labels and then by the property in the `where` clause. So, no more full scans.

The `EstimatedRows`, `Rows`, and `DbHits` values have significantly reduced and listed next are the new statistics:

- **EstimatedRows**: Earlier it was 1 and 9, and now it is 0 and 2
- **Rows**: Earlier it was 1 and 9, and now it is 1 and 2
- **DbHits**: Earlier it was 18 and 10, and now it is 4 and 3

Introducing a label has improved the overall throughput of our query by 50 percent. But still there is some more scope…

We discussed indexes in the previous sections, so now let's create an index on the label `FEMALE` and then run the same query again, without introducing any other criteria in the query. The output would be as follows:

Amazing!!!! Isn't it?

We have again improved the overall performance of the query by simply introducing an index over the label `FEMALE`.

Now the query filters are again changed and it is using **NodeIndexSeek**, which is further leveraging our newly created Indexes.

As a result, the total **DbHits** value has reduced to just 2 from 28 (18+10), which means that the total cost of the query has improved by 85 percent.

Though there is no golden rule for performance optimization, there could be many such scenarios where we can optimize our Cypher query by introducing the labels, indexes, or any additional information to help Neo4j filter the larger results early in the cycle, which in turn would reduce the overall cost of the query.

In this section, we have discussed various options and features provided by Neo4j for optimizing Cypher queries. We also discussed these by using appropriate examples and significantly improved the performance of our queries by introducing labels and indexes.

Summary

In this chapter, we have learned about the various ways of mutating (creating, updating, and deleting) nodes, labels, properties, and relationships in Neo4j. We also talked about the process of optimizing our Cypher queries using appropriate examples.

In the next chapter, we will discuss in detail Python and its integration with Neo4j using py2neo.

4
Getting Python and Neo4j to Talk Py2neo

Python is a widely used general-purpose and high-level programming language. The power of Python comes from the fact that it provides a high level of abstraction to the programmers from the concepts such as memory management, portability, and so on, which are the core features of Python, resulting in a readable, maintainable, and cleaner code. It emphasizes the speed of development where the programmers can pick up basic Python skills in a short time frame, and also describes the concepts and ideas in fewer lines of code in comparison to other programming languages such as C++ or Java.

Python is interpreted where it uses a just-in-time (also known as JIT) compiler named PyPy (`http://en.wikipedia.org/wiki/PyPy`) and provides faster development cycles, along with ease of programming and debugging to the programmers.

Python is interpreted, interactive, object-oriented, and supports multiple programming paradigms such as imperative, functional, procedural, structured, and aspect-oriented programming.

It also provides a wide variety of standard libraries and extensions, which makes it much more powerful in comparison to other programming languages.

Py2neo is another extension and client library for Python, specifically developed to work with Neo4j. It fully supports Neo4j 2.x and provides a comprehensive toolkit for working with all the core concepts of Neo4j, such as nodes, relationships, properties, labels, indexes, `MATCH`, and so on. It does not have any external dependencies and can be used as a standalone package with the basic Python installation.

In this chapter, we will discuss integration of Python and Neo4j using py2neo.

This chapter will cover the following topics:

- Installing and configuring py2neo
- Exploring py2neo APIs
- Creating a social network with py2neo
- Batch imports
- Unit testing

Installing and configuring py2neo

In this section, we will talk about installing and configuring py2neo and other resources required for quick development using APIs exposed by py2neo.

Py2neo is a simple, powerful, and pragmatic Python library that provides access to Neo4j via its RESTful Web service interface. It does not have external dependencies, and installation is simple and straightforward. The library is actively maintained on GitHub (`https://github.com/nigelsmall/py2neo`), regularly updated in the **Python Package Index** (**PPI**), and built uniquely for Neo4j in close association with its team and community.

Let's move forward and discuss the prerequisites and installation steps for py2neo.

Prerequisites

The following are the prerequisites required to install py2neo:

- **Python**: Python 3.4.x should be installed and configured. Perform the following steps in case you do not have Python installed:

    1. Depending upon your OS, download and install Python from `https://www.python.org/downloads/`.

    2. Update the `"PATH"` environment variable and append `"/usr/local/bin/python"` in Unix/Linux and `<$PYTHON_HOME>/Scripts` in Windows, where `"$PYTHON_HOME"` is the path of the root directory where Python is installed.

3. Open your console in Windows (or shell in Linux/Unix), type
   `python`, and you will see something like the following screenshot:

```
C:\myWork\instSoft\Python34\Scripts>python
Python 3.4.2 (v3.4.2:ab2c023a9432, Oct  6 2014, 22:15:05) [MSC v.1600 32 bit (Intel)] on win32
Type "help", "copyright", "credits" or "license" for more information.
>>> _
```

- **Integrated Development Environment (IDE)**: Install and configure your
  favorite IDE such as Eclipse (with PyDev plugin), PythonWin, or IDLE to
  write and execute Python scripts.

Going forward in this chapter, we will use Eclipse Luna (integrated with PyDev
plugin) and Windows as OS for all the given examples for Python and py2neo.

Installing py2neo

If you are familiar with Python, then you must be aware of PIP.

For those who are new to PIP, it is a packaging manager and installer for various
external and third-party Python packages/components that are maintained and
packaged by **Python Packaging Authority** (**PYPA**).

PIP is a recommended utility for installing all Python packages, and is more or
less a standard now for developers to be used for managing (installing, removing,
upgrading, and so on) all Python third-party components/packages.

PIP as an executable is already included and installed with Python 3.x. So our Python
installation already contains PIP.

For more information on PIP, refer to `https://pip.pypa.io/en/latest/index.html`.

It is very easy to install py2neo using PIP. Ensure that your system is connected to
the Internet and then execute the following command on your command prompt;
everything else will be handled by PIP itself:

```
pip install py2neo
```

Once this command is successfully completed, execute the following command to
see the list of packages installed by PIP:

```
pip list
```

You will see the result as shown in the following screenshot:

```
C:\myWork>pip install py2neo
Downloading/unpacking py2neo
  Running setup.py (path:C:\Users\sagupta\AppData\Local\Temp\pip_build_sagupta\py2neo\setup.py) egg_info for package py2
neo

Installing collected packages: py2neo
  Running setup.py install for py2neo
    building 'py2neo.packages.jsonstream.cjsonstream' extension

    Installing neobox-script.py script to C:\myWork\instSoft\Python34\Scripts
    Installing neobox.exe script to C:\myWork\instSoft\Python34\Scripts
    Installing neobox.exe.manifest script to C:\myWork\instSoft\Python34\Scripts
    Installing geoff-script.py script to C:\myWork\instSoft\Python34\Scripts
    Installing geoff.exe script to C:\myWork\instSoft\Python34\Scripts
    Installing geoff.exe.manifest script to C:\myWork\instSoft\Python34\Scripts
    Installing neoauth-script.py script to C:\myWork\instSoft\Python34\Scripts
    Installing neoauth.exe script to C:\myWork\instSoft\Python34\Scripts
    Installing neoauth.exe.manifest script to C:\myWork\instSoft\Python34\Scripts
    Installing neoget-script.py script to C:\myWork\instSoft\Python34\Scripts
    Installing neoget.exe script to C:\myWork\instSoft\Python34\Scripts
    Installing neoget.exe.manifest script to C:\myWork\instSoft\Python34\Scripts
    Installing cypher-script.py script to C:\myWork\instSoft\Python34\Scripts
    Installing cypher.exe script to C:\myWork\instSoft\Python34\Scripts
    Installing cypher.exe.manifest script to C:\myWork\instSoft\Python34\Scripts
Successfully installed py2neo
Cleaning up...

C:\myWork>pip list
pip (1.5.6)
py2neo (2.0.5)
setuptools (2.1)

C:\myWork>
```

The preceding illustration shows the output of the py2neo installation using PIP, and then the list of installed packages along with their versions.

Exploring the py2neo APIs

Py2neo provides various features and exposes a number of APIs to work with Neo4j. Let's discuss a few of the important APIs that we will use along with the examples in the upcoming sections.

Graph

Graph is one of the basic APIs and contains all the basic operations related to the graph database. It is a wrapper around the REST API (http://docs.neo4j.org/ chunked/stable/rest-api.html), exposed by Neo4j. It connects to the base URI of Neo4j, and then further discovers other REST endpoints exposed by Neo4j. Graph can be used to connect to the local or remote Neo4j server. It can also connect the Neo4j server running behind the firewall by providing the username in the URL itself. The following are the code snippets for using the Graph API and connecting to the Neo4j server:

- Connecting to the local Neo4j server:

  ```
  graph = Graph("http://localhost:7474/db/data/")
  ```

- Connecting to the remote Neo4j server:

  ```
  graph = Graph("http://<Domain_Name>:<PORT>/db/data/")
  ```

- Connecting to the Neo4j server behind the Firewall that requires HTTP authentication:

```
graph =
Graph("http://<username>:<password>@<Domain_Name>:<PORT>/db
/data/")
```

Apart from the preceding methods, it also exposes various other methods for creating/merging nodes and relationships, searching nodes, executing raw Cypher queries, and many more. We will look at all these methods in the upcoming sections.

Refer to `http://py2neo.org/2.0/essentials.html#the-graph` for the complete list of methods exposed by the Graph API.

Authentication

Neo4j 2.2.x introduces the optional username-password authentication mechanism for the REST APIs. It is enabled by default but can be disabled by modifying the property `"dbms.security.auth_enabled"` to `false` in `<$NEO4J_HOME>/conf/neo4j.properties`. The following are the two ways to authenticate the user before executing any rest APIs:

- Set the system environment variable `NEO4J_AUTH=<username>:<password>`, which will be automatically used by the REST APIs to authenticate the user
- Execute the `Py2neo.authentication` request with the username and password and authenticate the user

The following is the code snippet for authenticating the REST APIs using `Py2neo.authentication`:

```
import py2neo
from py2neo import Graph

if __name__ == '__main__':
    #First parameter is the URL, second is the username and third
is the password

    py2neo.authenticate("localhost:7474", "neo4j", "sumit")
    graph = Graph("http://localhost:7474/db/data/")
```

Py2neo also provides a command line utility `neoauth`, which can be used to either change the password or check whether there is any need to change the password (needed for new installations).

Execute the following command on your console for changing the password:

```
neoauth <username> <current-password> <new-password>
```

Execute the following command to check whether there is a need to change the password:

```
neoauth <username> <current-password/ default password>
```

> Refer to *Chapter 1, Your First Query with Neo4j*, section for more details on authentication for REST APIs.

Node

The Node class is more or less a wrapper class for Neo4j nodes, where we can define labels and properties for a node and also define utility methods for searching the nodes connected to the given node. It also provides features to work with Python collections for creating nodes.

Here is code snippet for creating nodes with properties and labels:

```python
import py2neo

from py2neo import Graph, Node

def creatNodeWithLabelProperties():
    print("Start - Creating Node with Label and Properties")
    # Authenticate the user using py2neo.authentication.
    # Ensure that you change the password 'sumit' as per your
database configuration.
    py2neo.authenticate("localhost:7474", "neo4j", "sumit")

    # Connect to Graph and get the instance of Graph
    graph = Graph("http://localhost:7474/db/data/")

    # Create Nodes, where all positional arguments to constructor
is Label.
    # And rest (keyword arguments) are Node Properties.
    #Below is a Node with 1 Label and 2 properties
    node1 = Node("FirstLabel", name="MyPythonNode1", neo4j_
version="2.2")
```

```
    #Below is a Node with 2 Label and 2 properties
    node2 = Node("FirstLabel", "SecondLabel",name="MyPythonNode2",
neo4j_version="2.2")

    #Now Use object of graph to create Node, the return type is a
python tuple
    #Multiple Nodes can be created in a single Graph command
    resultNodes = graph.create(node1, node2)
    #Iterate Over Tuple and print all the values in the Tuple
    for index in range(len(resultNodes)):
        print("Created Node - ", index, ", ", resultNodes[index])
    print("End - Creating Node with Label and Properties")

if __name__ == '__main__':
    print("Start Creating Nodes")
    creatNodeWithLabelProperties()
    print("End Creating Nodes")
```

The preceding piece of code creates two nodes and in the end also prints the nodes on the console, which are then created in the Neo4j server/database.

Perform the following steps to execute the code we just saw:

1. In case your Neo4j server is not started, open the console or command prompt and execute <$NEO4J_HOME>\bin\neo4j. This will start your Neo4j server.

2. Create a new file named CreateNode.py and copy the preceding code into that file.

3. Next, define the __main__ method and invoke this new method.

4. Save CreateNode.py, and execute "python CreateNode.py" on your command prompt or console from the location where you saved CreateNode.py.

And you are done !!!

You will see print messages, as defined in the above code, on the console. This is shown in the following illustration:

```
C:\myWork\MY-Books\PackPub\Neo4j-Python\Chapters\eclipseWorkspace\CH-4\src>python CreateNode.py
Start Creating Nodes
Start - Creating Node with Label and Properties
Created Node -  0 ,  (n0:FirstLabel {name:"MyPythonNode1",neo4j_version:"2.2"})
Created Node -  1 ,  (n3:FirstLabel:SecondLabel {name:"MyPythonNode2",neo4j_version:"2.2"})
End - Creating Node with Label and Properties
End Creating Nodes

C:\myWork\MY-Books\PackPub\Neo4j-Python\Chapters\eclipseWorkspace\CH-4\src>_
```

The previous illustration shows the results of `CreateNode.py`.

 In order to understand the preceding code, follow the comments provided before every line of the code. The same is followed for every code example.

The Node class also provides the `cast()` method, which can be used to create the instance of the Node class from other Python data types such as dictionary. We can create a node by providing a list of labels and dictionary.

Let's define one more method, that is `createNodeWithLabelPropertiesWithCast`, in the `CreateNode.py` file and invoke it from the `__main__` method. The content of this new method will be as follows:

```
def createNodeWithLabelPropertiesWithCast():
    print("Start - Creating Node with Label and Properties")
    # Authenticate the user using py2neo.authentication
    # Ensure that you change the password 'sumit' as per your
      database configuration.
    py2neo.authenticate("localhost:7474", "neo4j", "sumit")
    # Connect to Graph and get the instance of Graph
    graph = Graph("http://localhost:7474/db/data/")
    #Define a LIST of Labels
    labels = [ 'FirstLabel' ,'SecondLabel' ]

    #Define a DICTIONARY
    properties = {'name':'MyPythonNode2', 'neo4j_version':'2.2'}
    #CAST the node and invoke graph.create method.
    node = Node.cast(labels,properties)
    resultNode, = graph.create(node)
    print("Node - ", resultNode)
    print("End - Creating Node with Label and Properties")
```

The preceding method defines a list `labels` and dictionary `properties` datatypes and then leverages the `cast()` method to create a node.

We can also add or delete labels of a node by using `node.labels.add(<NewLabelName>)` or `node.labels.delete(<LabelName>)`, where `node` is the reference to the `Node` object that was created and `labels` is the method of the `Node` class. Finally, replace the text within the <...> with your new or existing label and call `node.push()` for publishing the changes from client to the server. We can also use `node.pull()` for pulling updates from the server to client.

Similar to nodes, we can also perform updates to properties by using `node.properties["<Name of Property>"] = "<New Value>"` and then invoking `node.push()` again for pushing updates to the server.

The Node class also defines a few more utility methods for searching the nodes related to the given nodes. These are as follows:

* `match`: Returns the iterator of all relationships attached to the given node
* `match_incoming`: Returns the iterator of all incoming relationships attached to the given node
* `match_outgoing`: Returns the iterator of all outgoing relationships attached to the given node

Refer to `http://py2neo.org/2.0/essentials.html#nodes` for the complete list of methods and their associated signatures/arguments exposed by the Node API.

Relationship

The Relationship class is more or less a wrapper class for Neo4j relationships, where we can define the relationship between two given nodes. It also defines the utility methods for searching the nodes connected to the given node, and provides features to define the properties of a given relationship.

The following is a code snippet for creating a relationship between three given nodes along with the properties for the given relationship:

```
import py2neo
from py2neo import Graph, Node, Relationship, Rev

def createRelationshipWithProperties():
    print("Start - Creating Relationships")
    # Authenticate the user using py2neo.authentication
    # Ensure that you change the password 'sumit' as per your
database configuration.
    py2neo.authenticate("localhost:7474", "neo4j", "sumit")
    # Connect to Graph and get the instance of Graph
    graph = Graph("http://localhost:7474/db/data/")
    # Create Node with Properties
    amy = Node("FEMALE", name="Amy")
    # Create one more Node with Properties
    kristine = Node("FEMALE",name="Kristine")
    # Create one more Node with Properties
    sheryl = Node("FEMALE",name="Sheryl")
```

```
    #Define an Object of relationship which depicts the relationship
between Amy and Kristine
    #We have also defined the properties of the relationship -
"since=2005"
    #By Default the direction of relationships is left to right,
i.e. the -->
    kristine_amy = Relationship(kristine,"FRIEND",amy,since=2005)

    #This relationship is exactly same as the earlier one but here
we are using "Rev"
    #"py2neo.Rev = It is used to define the reverse relationship
(<--) between given nodes
    amy_sheryl=Relationship(amy,Rev("FRIEND"),sheryl,since=2001)

    #Finally use graph Object and Create Nodes and Relationship
    #When we create Relationship between, then Nodes are also
created.
    resultNodes = graph.create(kristine_amy,amy_sheryl)
    #Print the results (relationships)
    print("Relationship Created - ",resultNodes)
if __name__ == '__main__':
    createRelationshipWithProperties()
```

This preceding piece of code creates three nodes — Amy, Kristine, and Sheryl, and defines the relationship between all these three nodes.

Perform the following steps to execute the code being discussed:

1. In case your Neo4j server is not started, open the console or command prompt and execute <$NEO4J_HOME>\bin\neo4j. This will start your Neo4j server.

2. Create a new file named CreateRelationship.py, save it, and execute "python CreateRelationship.py" on your command prompt or console from the location where you saved CreateRelationship.py.

And you are done!!!

You will see the print messages as defined in the previous code on the console.

Similar to nodes, relationship also defines the cast() method, which can create properties from the dictionary datatype.

Properties for a given relationship can be further read or modified using its index. For example, let's assume that we need to change the value of the property "since" to 2009 in the previous piece of code. This can be done using the following syntax:

```
kristine_amy["since"]=2009
```

You can also do it using the following syntax:

```
kristine_amy.properties["since"]=2009
```

Then finally invoke push() to send the modifications to the server:

```
kristine_amy.push()
```

Refer to http://py2neo.org/2.0/essentials.html#relationships for the complete list of methods exposed by the Relationship API.

Cypher

Py2neo provides a service wrapper for executing Cypher queries. The service wrapper also provides access to transactions and facilitates executing a single Cypher statement or streaming. The Cypher class is instantiated using the py2neo.Graph object and is available through the py2neo.Graph.cypher attribute.

There are multiple methods defined by the Cypher class. The following are a few of the common ones:

- py2neo.Graph.cypher.execute(...): This method executes a single Cypher query and returns a list of records wrapped in the py2neo.cypher. RecordList object. Another variation of the execute() method is execute_ one(), which returns the value from the first column of the first record fetched from the database.

- py2neo.Graph.cypher.stream(...): This method executes a single Cypher query and returns a result iterator. This method is different from others, as it incrementally handles the results of Cypher queries and batch requests as well as the results from a few other functions, such as match. In short, it provides access to HTTP Stream and we can iterate and fetch records one by one, which is unlike the other methods where we fetch the full result object.

- py2neo.Graph.cypher.run(...): It executes a single Cypher query and does not return anything.

Let's explore a few examples using the methods we just discussed.

Shown next is the code snippet for executing Cypher queries using the execute() method.

For brevity, we have moved the common piece of code for connecting graphs in a different method that would look something like the following:

```
import py2neo
from py2neo import Graph
def connectGraph():
    # Authenticate the user using py2neo.authentication
    # Ensure that you change the password 'sumit' as per your
database configuration.
    py2neo.authenticate("localhost:7474", "neo4j", "sumit")
    # Connect to Graph and get the instance of Graph
    graph = Graph("http://localhost:7474/db/data/")
    return graph
```

Now let's define another method, `executeSimpleCypherQuery()`, which will contain the following piece of code:

```
def executeSimpleCypherQuery():
    print("Start - execution of Simple Cypher Query")
    #Connect to Graph
    graph=connectGraph()
    #define and Execute a Cypher query which fetches all nodes
from the database.
    #object of 'cypher' is returned by 'graph' Object and then
further we use execute method Usually
    results = graph.cypher.execute("MATCH (n) return n.name as
name, labels(n) as labels")
    #Iterating ovver records and then printing the results.
    for index in range(len(results)):
        record = results[index]
        print("Printing Record = ",index," - Name =
",record.name,", Labels = ",record.labels)
    print("End - execution of Simple Cypher Query")
```

The preceding piece of code fetches all the nodes from the database and prints their label and property(name) on the console.

Perform the following steps to execute the code being discussed:

1. In case your Neo4j server is not started, open the console or command prompt and execute `<$NEO4J_HOME>\bin\neo4j`. This will start your neo4j server.

2. Create a new file by name of `ExecuteCypher.py` and copy the above code for both the methods, that is `connectGraph` and `executeSimpleCypherQuery()` in that file.

3. Next, define __main__ method and invoke `executeSimpleCypherQuery()`.

4. Save `ExecuteCypher.py` and execute `python ExecuteCypher.py` on your command prompt or console from the location where you saved `ExecuteCypher.py`.

And we are done!!!

You will see the print messages as defined in the preceding code on the console.

Following is the code snippet for using the `cypher.stream()` method for the same Cypher query that we executed in the `executeSimpleCypherQuery()` method:

```
def executeStreamingCypherQuery():

    print("Start - execution of Streaming Cypher Query")
    #Connect to Graph
    graph=connectGraph()
    #Call to cyhper.stream method which returns cypher.RecordStream
Object
    results = graph.cypher.stream("MATCH (n) return n.name as
name, labels(n) as labels")
    #Iterating over the RecordStream Object and print the results
    for recordStream in results:
        print("Printing Record - Name = ",recordStream.name,",
Labels = ",recordStream.labels)

    print("End - execution of Streaming Cypher Query")
```

The preceding piece of code also produces the same output as `executeSimpleCypherQuery()`. However, fundamentally it is different as it provides a stream of results rather than the complete result set in one single call.

Perform the following steps to execute the code being discussed:

1. In case your Neo4j server is not started, open the console or command prompt and execute `<$NEO4J_HOME>\bin\neo4j`. This will start your Neo4j server.

2. Add this new `executeStreamingCypherQuery()` method just below `executeSimpleCypherQuery()` in `ExecuteCypher.py`.

3. Next, invoke this method from the __main__ method.

4. Save `ExecuteCypher.py` and execute `python ExecuteCypher.py` on your command prompt or console from the location where you saved `ExecuteCypher.py`.

You will see the print messages as defined in the preceding code on the console.

Transactions

Cypher also provides support for transactions where you can execute multiple Cypher statements as a one unit of work, so that if something fails, you can rollback all previous statements and your database remains in a consistent state.

The following are a few of the common methods exposed by the `py2neo.cypher.CypherTransaction` class:

- `begin()`: Starts a transaction and returns the object of `py2neo.cypher.CypherTransaction`.
- `append()`: Appends the Cypher queries to the existing transactions.
- `commit()`: Sends all the Cypher queries in a transaction to the server and marks the transaction as completed.
- `rollback()`: Rollbacks all the changes within the current transaction.
- `process()`: Intermittently sends few transactions to the server and leaves the transaction open for further statements. It can be used to form a process where we can process multiple transactions in batches.

Following is the code snippet for using transactions for Cypher statements:

```
def executeCypherQueryInTransaction():
    print("Start - execution of Cypher Query in Transaction")
    #Connect to Graph
    graph=connectGraph()
    #begin a transaction
    tx = graph.cypher.begin()
    #Add statements to the transaction
    tx.append("CREATE (n:Node1{name:'John'}) RETURN n")
    tx.append("CREATE (n:Node1{name:'Russell'}) RETURN n")
    tx.append("CREATE (n:Node1{name:'Smith'}) RETURN n")
    #Finally commit the transaction and get results
    results = tx.commit()
    #Iterate over results and print the results
    for result in results:
        for record in result:
            print(record.n)
    print("End - execution of Cypher Query in Transaction")
```

Perform the following steps to execute the code being discussed:

1. In case your Neo4j server is not started, open the console or command prompt and execute `<$NEO4J_HOME>\bin\neo4j`. This will start your Neo4j server.

2. Add this new `executeCypherQueryInTransaction()` method just below `executeStreamingCypherQuery()` in `ExecuteCypher.py`.

3. Next, invoke this method from the `__main__` method.

4. Save `ExecuteCypher.py` and execute `"python CreateNode.py"` on your command prompt or console.

You will see the print messages as defined in the preceding code on the console.

Refer to `http://py2neo.org/2.0/cypher.html` for the complete list of methods exposed by Cypher API.

Paths

`py2neo.Path` works on relationships defined between the nodes. It provides the flexibility to create relationships between nodes that may be optionally bound to remote counterparts in a Neo4j database.

Apart from the common methods such as `push()`, `pull()`, `bound()`, and `unbind()`, Path defines a few new methods:

- `append(..)`: It is used to form a new path by connecting a new path or entity to the end of the existing path

- `preappend(..)`: It is used to form a new path by connecting a new path or entity to the beginning of the existing path

- `relationships(..)`: It is used to refer to a tuple of all the relationships in the given path

- `nodes(..)`: It is used to refer to a tuple of all the nodes in the given path

The following is an example that shows the usage of Path in creating relationships:

```
def createPaths():
    #Connect to Neo4j Database
    graph = connectGraph()
    #Let us define few Nodes
    bradley,matthew,lisa = Node(name="Bradley"),Node(name="Matthew"),
Node(name="Lisa")
    #Connect these Node and form a Path
    path_1 = Path(bradley,"Knows",matthew,Rev("Knows"),lisa)
```

```
    #Let us create this Path on the server
    graph.create(path_1)
    #Let us create some more Nodes
    john, annie, ripley = Node(name="John"), Node(name="Annie"),
Node(name="Ripley")
    #Define another Path for these New Nodes
    path_2 = Path(john,"Knows",annie,"Knows",ripley)
    #Now, we will join path_1 and path_2 using function append(),
and it will give us a new path
    path_3 = path_1.append("Knows",path_2)
    #Let us Create this new path in the server
    resultPath = graph.create(path_3)

    #Now we will print and see the results on the Console
    print("Print Raw Data")
    print("Nodes in the Path-1 = ",resultPath[0].nodes)
    print("Relationships in the Path-1 = ",resultPath[0].
relationships)

    print("Print - All Relationships")
    for rels in resultPath[0].relationships:
        print(rels)

if __name__ == '__main__':
    createPaths()
```

Perform the following steps to execute the code being discussed:

1. In case your Neo4j server is not started, open the console or command prompt and execute <$NEO4J_HOME>\bin\neo4j. This will start your Neo4j server.

2. Create a new file ExplorePaths.py and copy the preceding code into that file.

3. Define the connectGraph() method in ExplorePaths.py just above createPaths() which connects to the server and returns the object of graph. Alternatively, you can also copy this method from previous examples.

4. Save ExplorePaths.py and execute "python ExplorePaths.py" on your command prompt or console from the location where you saved ExplorePaths.py.

You will see the print messages as defined in the above code on the console.

Refer to http://py2neo.org/2.0/essentials.html#paths for the complete list of methods exposed by the Path API.

In this section, we discussed about the important APIs of py2neo that are used to interact with the Neo4j database. Let's move forward; in the next section we will create the social network data using these APIs.

Creating a social network with py2neo

In the previous section, we saw the important APIs exposed by py2neo along with examples for each of them. In this section, we will further use these APIs and see their practical implementations in real-world scenarios.

Let's recreate the social network data which we created using Cypher in *Chapter 2*, *Querying the Graph with Cypher*, using various APIs and methods exposed by py2neo.

First and foremost, we will clean up our database, so perform the following steps to do that:

1. Open your console or command prompt and execute `<$NEO4J_HOME>\bin\ neo4jshell`.

2. Execute the following Cypher queries to delete the data from Neo4j database:
   ```
   OPTIONAL MATCH (n)-[r]-(n1) delete r,n.n1;
   MATCH n delete n;
   ```

Next we need to write some Python and code using py2neo to create a graph, which will look something like the following figure:

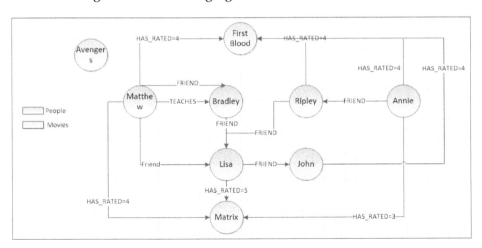

The previous illustration shows the layout of the data model which we will be creating using py2neo APIs.

Perform the following steps to create the social network data using py2neo:

1. Create a Python class and name it `CreateSocialNetworkData.py`.

2. Next, edit `CreateSocialNetworkData.py` and define the following functions:

   ◦ `connectGraph`: This will contain the code for connecting the server and returning the object of the graph, which is similar to what we created/used in previous examples.

   ◦ `createPople`: This will contain the code for creating the people in our social network data using Node API of py2neo, and will return the object of dictionary with all the `People` nodes:

   ```
   def createPeople(self,graph):
           print("Creating People")
           bradley = Node('MALE','TEACHER',name='Bradley',
   surname='Green', age=24, country='US')
           matthew = Node('MALE','STUDENT',name='Matthew',
   surname='Cooper', age=36, country='US')
           lisa = Node('FEMALE',name='Lisa', surname='Adams',
   age=15, country='Canada')
           john = Node('MALE',name='John', surname='Godman',
   age=24, country='Mexico')
           annie = Node('FEMALE',name='Annie', surname='Behr',
   age=25, country='Canada')
           ripley = Node('MALE',name='Ripley',
   surname='Aniston', country='US')
           graph.create(bradley,matthew,lisa,john,annie,ripley)
           print("People Created")
           #Create a Dictionary and return back the nodes for
   further operations
           people =
   {'bradley':bradley,'matthew':matthew,'lisa':lisa,'john':john
   ,'annie':annie,'ripley':ripley}
           return people
   ```

   ◦ `createFriends(..)`: It will contain the code for creating relationships between the people we created in `createPople()` using the `Path` API of py2neo, and will further return all the paths created between people:

   ```
   def createFriends(self,graph,people):
           print("Creating Relationships between People")

           path_1 =
   Path(people['bradley'],'FRIEND',people['matthew'],'FRIEND',p
   eople['lisa'],'FRIEND',people['john'])
   ```

```
        path_2 = path_1.prepend(people['lisa'],Rev('FRIE
ND'))
        path_3 =
Path(people['annie'],'FRIEND',people['ripley'],'FRIEND',peo
ple['lisa'])
        path_4 =
Path(people['bradley'],'TEACHES',people['matthew'])
        friendsPath = graph.create(path_2,path_3,path_4)
        print("Finished Creating Relationships between
People")
    return friendsPath
```

° createMovies(..): This function is similar to createPople; the only difference is that it will create the movies and will return the object of dictionary with all the Movie nodes:

```
def createMovies(self,graph):
        print("Creating Movies")
        firstBlood = Node('MOVIE',name='First Blood')
        avengers = Node('MOVIE',name='Avengers')
        matrix = Node('MOVIE',name='matrix')
        graph.create(firstBlood,avengers,matrix)
        print("Movies Created")
        movies =
{'firstBlood':firstBlood,'avengers':avengers,'matrix':matr
ix}
        return movies
```

° rateMovies(..): This function is similar to createFriends; the only difference is that it will create the relationship between the People and Movies nodes using the HAS_RATED relationship. It will use the Relationship API of py2neo to create the relationship:

```
def rateMovies(self,graph,movies,people):
        print("Start Rating the Movies")

        matthew_firstBlood =
Relationship(people['matthew'],'HAS_RATED',movies['firstBloo
d'],ratings=4)
        john_firstBlood =
Relationship(people['john'],'HAS_RATED',movies['firstBlood'
],ratings=4)
        annie_firstBlood =
Relationship(people['annie'],'HAS_RATED',movies['firstBlood
'],ratings=4)
        ripley_firstBlood =
Relationship(people['ripley'],'HAS_RATED',movies['firstBlood
'],ratings=4)
```

```
        lisa_avengers =
Relationship(people['lisa'],'HAS_RATED',movies['avengers'],
ratings=5)
        matthew_avengers =
Relationship(people['matthew'],'HAS_RATED',movies['avengers
'],ratings=4)
        annie_avengers =
Relationship(people['annie'],'HAS_RATED',movies['avengers']
,ratings=3)
        moviesPath =
graph.create(matthew_firstBlood,john_firstBlood,annie_
firstBlood,ripley_firstBlood,lisa_avengers,matthew_
avengers,annie_avengers)
        print("Finished Rating the Movies")
        return moviesPath
```

3. Now, we will define a `__main__` method, create an object of class `CreateSocialNetworkData`, and invoke all the previous methods in the same sequence as they are defined.

4. Next, save `CreateSocialNetworkData.py` and execute Python `CreateSocialNetworkData.py` on your command prompt or console from the location where you saved `CreateSocialNetworkData.py`.

And we are done!!!

You will see the same graph in your Neo4j database that we created in *Chapter 2, Querying the Graph with Cypher*, using Cypher.

Batch imports

`Py2neo.batch` provides the Batch API, which is a wrapper around the Neo4j REST Batch API (`http://neo4j.com/docs/stable/rest-api-batch-ops.html`).

The Batch API in py2neo or in Neo4j is designed to wrap multiple and varied types of read, write, update, and delete REST requests in a single transaction. Though it seems to be a good choice to use batch operations, it is not recommended for new use cases that are built for Neo4j 2.0+. For example, schemas, and labels are not supported by the Batch API.

Neo4j 2.0 introduces a new Cypher HTTP Transactional endpoint that executes multiple Cypher statements into a single request and that too in a transaction (`http://neo4j.com/docs/milestone/rest-api-transactional.html`). It is strongly recommended to use this new API for all use cases developed on Neo4j 2.0 and above. We have seen an example of this while we were discussing the Cypher API in the *Exploring py2neo APIs* section.

The following is the code snippet for working with the Batch API:

```
def createAndExecuteBatchRequest(self):
    # Authenticate the user using py2neo.authentication
    # Ensure that you change the password 'sumit' as per your
database configuration.
    py2neo.authenticate("localhost:7474", "neo4j", "sumit")
    # Connect to Graph and get the instance of Graph
    graph = Graph("http://localhost:7474/db/data/")

    #Get the instance of Write Batch request
    batch = WriteBatch(graph)
    #Create a Node
    daisy = Node(name='Daisy')
    # Now invoke create method on batch. It also shows
another way of creating the Node
    batch.create({'name':'Hana'})
    batch.create(daisy)
    #Create a relationships between the Nodes
    batch.create((0,Rev('KNOWS'),1))
    #Finally submit the Nodes
    batch.submit()
```

The preceding piece of code creates two nodes and then further creates the relationship between those two nodes.

Refer to http://py2neo.org/2.0/batch.html for the complete list of classes and methods exposed by the Batch API.

Perform the following steps to execute the code being discussed:

1. In case your Neo4j server is not started, open the console or command prompt and execute <$NEO4J_HOME>\bin\neo4j. This will start your Neo4j server.

2. Create a new class ExploreBatch.py and add the preceding piece of code just below the constructor.

3. Next, invoke this new method from the __main__ method.

4. Save ExploreBatch.py and run this class by executing "python ExecuteCypher.py" on the command prompt or console.

In this section, we discussed about the Batch API provided by py2neo for executing multiple requests into a single, transactional Batch request. Let's move forward towards the next section and discuss unit testing of our newly created data model.

Unit testing

One of the core objectives of Python is to bring in speed of development where developers can implement functional requirements in the shortest possible time and with fewer lines of code, which is in sync and embraces popular development models such as Agile (`http://en.wikipedia.org/wiki/Agile_software_development`) or Extreme Programming (`http://en.wikipedia.org/wiki/Extreme_programming`).

But at the same time it is also important to ensure that adding new code does not break the integrity of the system. This is only possible with an efficient/effective set of automated unit test cases.

Unit testing is an important aspect of any development lifecycle. It not only involves testing the expected outcome but at the same time it also tests unexpected conditions/scenarios and the behavior of the system.

Unit tests are an integral part of any test strategy. They are intended to break the entire codebase into several pieces and ensure that each piece or unit of work is producing the expected results. A good test suite is also used later as a regression test suite in the development cycle.

Even in some development models such as **Test Drive Development** (TDD) (`http://en.wikipedia.org/wiki/Test-driven_development`), it is advised to write a failing automated test case that defines a desired functionality or outcome, then further produces the minimum amount of code to pass that test, and in the end refactors the new code to the acceptable standards.

Neo4j or graph data models perfectly fit into this scenario as these models are evolving and are developed over a period of time. The code that supports these evolving models is highly agile and is constantly changing, so naturally it becomes imperative to write effective and efficient unit test suites.

Python comes with a unit testing framework, popularly known as PyUnit, that is a Python version of Junit (`http://junit.org/`). Junit is for Java and PyUnit is for Python.

Let's move forward and discuss the process of creating unit tests for our social network data.

Perform the following steps to create a unit test that verifies that nodes are created and are available on the server:

1. Create a package by the name of `test` and within this package create a file named `TestSocialNetworkData.py`.

2. Next, edit `TestSocialNetworkData.py` and add the `TestingGraph` class, which extends `unittest.TestCase`. This class will define the `testServerConnection()` method, which will test the connection with the Neo4j server and looks like the following:

```
import unittest

from CreateSocialNetworkData import *

class TestingGraph(unittest.TestCase):

    def testServerConnection (self):
        graph = CreateSocialNetworkData.connectGraph(self)
        #Check whether Graph Object is created and bound to
the remote entities
        self.assertTrue (graph.bound)
```

In the preceding test method we are invoking the `connectGraph()` method of the class `CreateSocialNetworkData` and then using assertions (`assertTrue`) to check that the graph is bounded to the remote entities, residing in the Neo4j server/database.

3. Next, edit `TestSocialNetworkData.py` and add the class `TestingNodes` which extends `unittest.TestCase`. This class will define two methods — `testLabelCount()` and `testIndividualNodes()`. The `testLabelCount()` method will test the count of total unique labels attached to all the nodes, which should be equivalent to the count of the expected labels, and `testIndividualNodes()` will check whether the individual nodes in the server are equivalent to the expected nodes created by our `CreateSocialNetworkData` class. The following is the code snippet for the `TestingNodes` class:

```
class TestingNodes(unittest.TestCase):
    def setUp(self):
        py2neo.authenticate("localhost:7474", "neo4j",
"sumit")
        # Connect to Graph and get the instance of Graph
        graph = Graph("http://localhost:7474/db/data/")
        self.graph = graph
```

```
def tearDown(self):
    self.graph.unbind()

def testLabelCount(self):
    results = self.graph.cypher.execute("MATCH (n)
return count(DISTINCT labels(n)) as countLabel")
    #We should have only 5 Labels "FEMALE(2) MALE(4)
MOVIE(3) STUDENT(1) TEACHER(1)"
    self.assertEqual(5, results[0].countLabel)

def testIndividualNodes(self):
    #Define a Node which we need to check
    bradley = Node('MALE','TEACHER',name='Bradley',
surname='Green', age=24, country='US')
    #Now get the Node from server
    results = self.graph.cypher.execute("MATCH (n)
where n.name='Bradley' return n as bradley")
    #Both Nodes should be equal
    self.assertEqual(results[0].bradley,bradley)
```

4. Next we will test the paths (relationships). Edit TestSocialNetworkData.py and add the TestingPaths class which extends unittest.TestCase. Apart from the setUp() and tearDown() methods, which remain the same as we created in class TestingNode, this class will define two new methods— testPathFRIENDExists and testPathTEACHESExists(). Both these will check the existence of relationship between the nodes in Neo4j server/ database, which was created by our CreateSocialNetworkData class. The following is the code snippet for these two new methods:

```
def testPathFRIENDExists(self):
    #Query whether there are Nodes linked with
Relationship - FRIEND
    results = self.graph.cypher.execute("MATCH
(n{name:'Bradley'})-[r:FRIEND]->(n1{name:'Matthew'}) return
count(r) as countPath")
    #Ensure that count=1. Not more, neither less
    self.assertEqual(1,results[0].countPath)

def testPathTEACHESFRIENDExists(self):
    #Query whether there are Nodes linked with
Relationship - TEACHES
    results = self.graph.cypher.execute("MATCH
(n{name:'Bradley'})-[r:TEACHES]->(n1{name:'Matthew'})
return count(r) as countPath")
    #Ensure that count=1. Not more, neither less
    self.assertEqual(1,results[0].countPath)
```

5. Now, to execute these test cases, we will define a test suite that will execute all the test cases of our social network data in one go. Create a new Python module outside the `test` package, name it as `ExecuteUnitTests.py`, and add the following code:

```
from test import *

if __name__ == '__main__':
    baseTestsuite = unittest.TestLoader().loadTestsFromTestCase(Te
stingGraph)
    nodeTestsuite = unittest.TestLoader().loadTestsFromTestCase(Te
stingNodes)
    pathTestsuite = unittest.TestLoader().loadTestsFromTestCase(Te
stingPaths)
    baseTestsuite.addTest(nodeTestsuite)
    baseTestsuite.addTest(pathTestsuite)
    unittest.TextTestRunner(verbosity=2).run(baseTestsuite)
```

And we are done!!!

Now open your console or command prompt and execute `py ExecuteUnitTests.py` from the location where you saved it, and you will see the results on the console. You can add more test cases or assertions for testing your social network data and make it as robust as it should be.

We should also remember that it is good to have a unit test case but it should be intelligent enough to cover all scenarios of your codebase.

 There are other testing frameworks that can be used to perform unit testing, such as `http://pytest.org/`

In this section, we discussed about the importance of unit testing and also the process of defining the unit tests for Neo4j using PyUnit.

Summary

In this chapter, we learned about py2neo as a Python framework for working with Neo4j. We talked about various APIs of py2neo and also created social network data using the same APIs. We also discussed about the Batch imports provided by py2neo and in the end we talked about the process of unit testing of Neo4j graphs using PyUnit.

In the next chapter, we will discuss in detail about the RESTful services with Flask and py2neo.

5
Build RESTful Service with Flask and Py2neo

The emergence of cloud-computing, and the growing interest in web-hosted applications and **Representational State Transfer** (**REST**) based web-services (also known as RESTful services) have gained popularity that can help both in the development of rich user interface clients calling into remote servers and in the development of actual servers for manipulating data structures in a client application (written in any language) or directly in the browser.

Representational State Transfer is a new software architecture style for networked systems consisting of clients and servers.

REST recommends you develop requests and responses around the transfer of representation of resources. A resource can be essentially any coherent and meaningful concept that is addressed. A representation of a resource is typically a document that captures the current or intended state of the resource.

Flask (`http://flask.pocoo.org/`) is a lightweight Python-based "microframework" (`http://en.wikipedia.org/wiki/Microframework`) available under the BSD license (`http://en.wikipedia.org/wiki/BSD_licenses`) for developing web-based applications in Python. Flask is simpler and lighter to use as compared to other Python-based web frameworks but contains all the required features to develop small but powerful applications. Flask is extensible and provides a variety of extensions, which further helps in developing robust applications.

Flask-RESTful (`https://pypi.python.org/pypi/Flask-RESTful`) is one such Python-based extension that helps in developing and exposing REST-based APIs using Python.

In the last chapter, we discussed about the integration of Neo4j and py2neo, and in this chapter, we will discuss Flask as a framework for building and exposing RESTful services using py2neo and Neo4j.

This chapter will cover the following points:

- Introduction and installation of Flask
- Setting up web applications using Flask and Flask-RESTful
- REST APIs for social network data using py2neo

Introducing (and installing) Flask

In this section, we will talk about installing and configuring Flask and its extensions required for quick development of web applications.

Python is known for its fast development, easy syntax, and clean code; it provides the flexibility for developing applications within minutes, and without worrying about complex deployment instructions. The same ideology is leveraged within the Python web frameworks where we have a variety of framework choices for developing varied kinds of application, ranging from small to complex enterprise systems. Flask is one such Python-based, extensible, web-based framework and provides quicker development of small and medium-sized but powerful applications.

It is based on Werkzeug (`http://werkzeug.pocoo.org/`)and Jinja2 (`http://quintagroup.com/cms/python/jinja2`), and is inspired by Sinatra Ruby framework (`http://www.sinatrarb.com/`).

Flask is called a "microframework" because it keeps the core simple but extensible. It has no database abstraction layer, form validation, or any other components where pre-existing third-party libraries provide common functions. However, Flask is extensible and supports the development of custom extensions over the core framework for adding application features as if they were implemented in Flask itself. Extensions exist for RESTful services, i18n, NoSQL databases such as CouchDB (`http://couchdb.apache.org/`), authentication/authorizations, and many more. A few of the notable features of Flask are as follows:

- In-built development server for hosting web applications and debugger
- Integrated support for unit testing
- RESTful style of request dispatching

- Jinja2 templating
- Support for secure cookies (client-side sessions)
- 100 percent WSGI 1.0 (`http://wsgi.readthedocs.org/`) compliant
- Compatible with Google App Engine
- Extensive documentation and provision of a wide range of extensions (`http://flask.pocoo.org/extensions/`)

Let's move ahead and learn about the installation of Flask.

Flask and its extensions are hosted in PyPI, so it can be installed via PIP itself. Execute the following command on your console or command prompt for installing Flask and its RESTful extension for developing RESTful services:

```
pip install flask Flask-RESTful
```

Now sit back and relax! It will take a minute or so, depending upon your internet speed, for PIP to download, install, and configure Flask, its dependencies, and its RESTful extension.

As soon as the process is successfully completed, execute `pip list` to see the list of all Python extensions installed, configured, and ready to use.

```
C:\>pip list
aniso8601 (0.92)
Flask (0.10.1)
Flask-RESTful (0.3.2)
itsdangerous (0.24)
Jinja2 (2.7.3)
MarkupSafe (0.23)
pip (1.5.6)
py2neo (2.0.5)
pytz (2014.10)
setuptools (2.1)
six (1.9.0)
Werkzeug (0.10.1)
```

And we are done!!!

Nothing else is required with respect to configurations. PIP has done all the configurations and now we can start developing web applications using Flask.

Let's move on to the next section and discuss the development of web-based applications using Flask.

Setting up web applications with Flask and Flask-RESTful

In this section, we will talk about the basics of developing web applications using Flask and Flask-RESTful.

Your first Flask application

As we discussed earlier, Flask is simple and straightforward. There are no complex rules or steps for developing web applications in Flask.

Perform the following steps to create your first web application using Flask:

1. Create a module and name it `FlaskWebApp.py`.

2. Edit `FlaskWebApp.py` and add the following code:

```
from flask import Flask
webapp = Flask(__name__)

@webapp.route("/")
def hello():
    return " Hello World!"

if __name__ == '__main__':
    webapp.run(host='0.0.0.0',port=8999,debug=True)
```

3. Next, open your console or command prompt and execute `py FlaskWebApp.py`. You will see something like the next screenshot:

```
C:\myWork\MY-Books\PackPub\Neo4j-Python\Chapters\eclipseWorkspace\CH-5-Flask-OGM\src\FlaskWebApp.py
 * Running on http://localhost:8999/ (Press CTRL+C to quit)
 * Restarting with stat
|
```

And we are done!!!

Your first application is up and running on port `8999`.

Next, you can open your web browser and type `http://localhost:8999` in the URL navigation bar. You will see `"Hello World!"` printed on the browser.

Let's understand the preceding piece of code:

- `from flask import Flask`: This is the first statement in our code where we import the class `Flask` from the package `flask`.

- `webapp = Flask(__name__)`: In this statement, we have created an object of the class `Flask` with a parameter `__name__`. The object of `Flask` acts as a nucleus or a registry for accessing the view functions, the URL rules, template configuration, and much more. The argument `__name__` is the name of the application of module where all the web application resources such as templates, static files, and so on are available. In our case it is a single module, so we can just provide `__name__` as a parameter.

  For more information, have a look at the Flask documentation at `http://flask.pocoo.org/docs/0.10/api/#flask.Flask`.

  > It is advisable to instantiate object of Flask object in `init.py`, so that it is available to packages and sub-packages.

- `@webapp.route("/")`: This statement defines a URL pattern which would be added to the Flask URL registry. Just below this `route` method, we need to define the function that will be invoked as soon as the user requests the provided URL pattern, which in our case is `def hello():`. This method is also called the view function and it needs to return the content which needs to be displayed to the user.

- `webapp.run(host='0.0.0.0',port=8999,debug=True)`: Lastly, we execute our webapp by invoking the `run` method of Flask in our `__main__` method with three parameters:
    - `HOST`: This is the IP address or domain name that will be used to serve the user request for the web application. It defaults to `127.0.0.1` and defines the value to `0.0.0.0`, so that Flask can listen on all network interfaces, not just on localhost.
    - `PORT`: This is the port number of the webserver, which is by default `5000`.
    - `debug=TRUE` or `debug=FALSE`: If set to `TRUE` then it will print the complete stack trace of the errors, else it will just print the error.

Flask also provides the flexibility to define the static and dynamic content.

Let's see the process of presenting our user with the static HTML files or dynamic content that can produce results based on user input.

Displaying static content

Web applications also need static files such as HTML, JavaScript, or CSS files. Usually, the static files are served by the web servers but Flask also provides the additional feature to store and serve them.

We need to create a `static` folder next to our module and then the files within the `static` folder can be accessed using `/static/<name of file>`.

Perform the following steps to create a function in our `FlaskWebApp` that renders the static files:

1. Edit your `FlaskWebApp` and modify the import statements to add the `redirect` function from the `flask` package and `url_for` from `flask.helpers`. Your import statements will look as follows:

   ```
   from flask import Flask, redirect
   from flask.helpers import url_for
   ```

2. Next, define a `static` folder just parallel to your `FlaskWebApp` and within the `static` folder, add an HTML file. Name it as `staticHTMLFile.html` with some HTML content.

3. Now define a new function in your `FlaskWebApp` that will serve this HTML file, and will look like the following:

   ```
   @webapp.route("/static", methods=['GET'])
   def showStaticFiles():
       return
   redirect(url_for('static',filename='staticHTMLFile.html'))
   ```

And we are done!!!

Open your browser and in the URL navigation bar enter `http://localhost:8999/static/`. You will see the static content defined in the HTML `staticHTMLFile.html` file.

In this new method we have used three new features:

- `methods=["GET"]`: Within the `route` function, we can also provide the constraints with respect to the type of HTTP method served by this method/function. For example, we have defined that our function `showStaticFiles` will be executed only if the HTTP method is of type `GET`. You can also provide multiple HTTP methods separated by a comma.

- `url_for`: This function is used for computing the URL of the provided endpoint. In our case, we provided the name of the folder and name of the file for which URL needs to be generated.

- `redirect`: This function redirects the user/client to the targeted URL/location.

 `methods=['GET']` of the `route()` function can also be used to develop RESTful web services. Refer to `http://blog.miguelgrinberg.com/post/designing-a-restful-api-with-python-and-flask`.

Displaying dynamic content

Similar to static content, we can also process and display dynamic content in Flask.

Flask leverages Jinja2 (`http://jinja.pocoo.org/2/`) templating engine for rendering templates or dynamic content.

Let's enhance our `FlaskWebApp` and add features to process and show some dynamic content.

Perform the following steps to add capabilities in our WebApp for processing dynamic content:

1. Create a folder `templates` parallel to the folder `static`.

2. Create a new file in the `templates` folder and give it the name `dynamicTemplate.html`.

3. Add the following content in your `dynamicTemplate.html`:

```
<!DOCTYPE html>
<html><head><meta charset="ISO-8859-1">
<title>Dynamic Template</title>
</head>
<body>
<h1>Hello {{ name }}</h1>
</body></html>
```

In this template, we have defined `{{name}}` as the variable that will be replaced by the value given by the user.

4. Next, edit your `FlexWebApp` and define a new import statement as follows:

```
from flask.templating import render_template
```

5. Next, just above the __main__ function, define a new function the following:

```
@webapp.route("/showDynamic/<name>")
def renderDynamicContent(name=None):
    return
render_template('dynamicTemplate.html',name=name)
```

6. In this function, we are defining a different URL pattern in `@webapp.route` that ends with `<name>`. This signifies that, along with the URL, the user will pass some additional data which will be further processed by the function `renderDynamicContent()`. Next we are passing the content provided by the user to our dynamic template by using `render_template(...)`. Now the Jinja templating engine will replace the value of `name` in our `dynamicTemplate.html` with the actual value passed on by the user.

7. Next, open a new browser and in the browser navigation bar enter the URL `http://localhost:8999/showDynamic/Sumit`. You will see the dynamic content displayed on your browser.

8. You can use all programming constructs in your templates. For example, replace the content of the `<body></body>` tag of your `dynamicTemplate.html` with the following, so that it can show some specific content based on the value of the variable passed on by the user:

```
<body>
{%if name == 'Sumit'%}
<h1>Hello {{ name }} - Author of  "Building Python Web Apps
with Neo4j"!!!</h1>
{% else %}
<h2>Hello {{ name }} !!!</h2>
{% endif %}
</body>
```

Refer to the `http://jinja.pocoo.org/docs/dev/api/` for the complete list of programming constructs and syntax available in Jinja2.

Flask provides access to all basic functionality of a web application, where you can access the user session, request, response, context, and so on.

Refer to official documentation available at `http://flask.pocoo.org/docs/0.10/quickstart/#` for more information about the features provided by Flask.

In this section, we have discussed the basics of developing web applications with Flask. Let's move forward and understand about creating/exposing REST APIs using the Flask-RESTful extension.

Your first Flask RESTful API

In this section, we will discuss and develop RESTful APIs using Flask-RESTful extension.

In recent years, RESTful APIs have become a default and standard architectural design pattern for web services. RESTful APIs are developed upon the standard HTTP protocol, which defines that all types of user request can be served by the default HTTP methods and data is exchanged using JSON (`http://en.wikipedia.org/wiki/JSON`), which is lightweight, simple, and easy to understand.

Refer to `http://en.wikipedia.org/wiki/Hypertext_Transfer_Protocol#Request_methods` for more information on the type of HTTP methods.

Let's move forward and develop our first RESTful service.

Perform the following steps to create RESTful API:

1. Create a new module `FlaskRestfulService.py`.

2. Edit `FlaskRestfulService.py` and define the following import statements:

    ```
    from flask import Flask
    from flask_restful import Api, Resource
    ```

3. Now, in `FlaskRestfulService.py`, just below the `import` statement, create an object of Flask and API:

    ```
    webapp = Flask(__name__)
    api = Api(webapp)
    ```

4. Next, define a class `HelloWorld(Resource)` in your `FlaskRestfulService.py`.

5. Just above the class definition, define `@api.resource('/hello')`, which will bind your class with an endpoint `http://<host>:<port>/hello`.

     You can also bind the REST endpoint by using `api.add_resource(..)` in your `__main__` method.

6. Next, within `HelloWorld`, define functions for each HTTP method. For example, for HTTP GET, you need to define the following:

    ```
    def get(self):
    return 'Hello - this is GET'
    ```

    Similarly, define the functions for POST, PUT, and DELETE.

7. Next, define a __main__ method:

```
if __name__ == '__main__':
    webapp. run(debug=True)
```

8. Now open the command prompt or console and start your RESTful service by executing `py FlaskRestfulService.py`.

9. Now open any tool such as SOAP-UI (`http://www.soapui.org/`), which provides creation and execution of REST calls and execute the following request:

   ◦ Request method type: `POST` or `GET` or `PUT` or `DELETE`

   ◦ Request URL: `http://localhost:5000/hello`

   ◦ Request headers: `Accept: application/json; charset=UTF-8` and `Content-Type: application/json`

That's all we have to do !!!

Based on your request method type, the Flask-RESTful will invoke and process the corresponding method of your class `HelloWorld` and show the results. For example, if you use `GET` then `def get(self):` will be executed.

JSON processing

Flask also provides a feature for receiving, processing, and returning back the JSON response. It exposes methods such as `request.get_json()` for retrieving JSON data from a request and `flask.jsonify(..)` for transforming a response into JSON format and further sending it back to the users.

For example, let's track the number of users invoking our RESTful service, which we developed in the previous example. Perform the following steps for enhancing our `HelloWorld` class for tracking user visits:

1. Edit the module `FlaskRRestfulService.py` and import `flask.jsonify` and `flask.request`. Also define a global variable by the name of `noOfVisitors = 0`.

2. Next, modify your `HelloWorld.post()` method and add the following code for reading JSON data and tracking the number of visitors:

```
def post(self):
        #Retrieve the JSON data from the Request and store it in
local variable
        jsonData = request.get_json(cache=False)
        #Iterate over the JSON Data and print the data on console
        for key in jsonData:
            import json
            print(json.dumps(jsonData, indent=2, sort_keys=True) )

        #reference to Global Variable
        global noOfVisitors
        #Adding 1 to the global Variable
        noOfVisitors = noOfVisitors + 1
        #Converting the response to JSON and returning back to
user
        return jsonify(totalVisits = noOfVisitors)
```

3. Next, save `FlaskRRestfulService.py`. Restart your application by first stopping it by pressing *Ctrl + C* and then executing `py FlaskRRestfulService.py` on your console or command prompt.

And we are done!!

Now open any tool such as SOAP-UI (`http://www.soapui.org/`), which provides creation and execution of REST calls, and execute the following request:

- Request method type: `POST`
- Request URL: `http://localhost:5000/hello`
- Request headers: `Accept: application/json; charset=UTF-8` and `Content-Type: application/json`
- JSON request:

```
{
    "book": "Building Python Web Apps with Neo4j",
    "Author": "Sumit",
    "publication": "PackPub"
}
```

You will get the JSON response back stating the number of visits of this REST service. Also, on your console you will see the attributes of the JSON request sent across by the user.

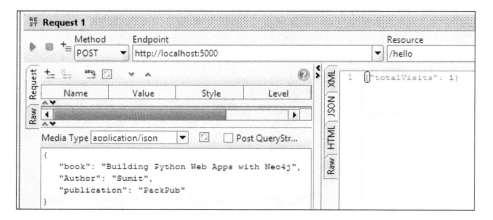

The preceding screenshot shows the results of the JSON response received from our RESTful service.

In this section, we talked about developing web-based applications using Flask. Further, we also discussed about exposing the RESTful service using Flask-RESTful extension. Let's move on to the next section and develop some useful REST-based services on our social network data for performing CRUD and search operations, using Flask-RESTful and py2neo.

REST APIs for social network data using py2neo

In this section, we will discuss and develop RESTful APIs for performing CRUD and search operations over our social network data, using Flask-RESTful extension and py2neo extension—**Object-Graph Mapper (OGM)**. Let's move forward to first quickly talk about the OGM and then develop full-fledged REST APIs over our social network data.

ORM for graph databases py2neo – OGM

We discussed about the py2neo in *Chapter 4, Getting Python and Neo4j to Talk Py2neo*. In this section, we will talk about one of the py2neo extensions that provides high-level APIs for dealing with the underlying graph database as objects and its relationships.

Object-Graph Mapping (`http://py2neo.org/2.0/ext/ogm.html`) is one of the popular extensions of py2neo and provides the mapping of Neo4j graphs in the form of objects and relationships. It provides similar functionality and features as **Object Relational Model (ORM)** available for relational `databases py2neo.ext.ogm.` `Store(graph)` is the base class which exposes all operations with respect to graph data models. Following are important methods of `Store` which we will be using in the upcoming section for mutating our social network data:

- `Store.delete(subj)`: It deletes a node from the underlying graph along with its associated relationships. `subj` is the entity that needs to be deleted. It raises an exception in case the provided entity is not linked to the server.

- `Store.load(cls, node)`: It loads the data from the database `node` into `cls`, which is the entity defined by the data model.

- `Store.load_related(subj, rel_type, cls)`: It loads all the nodes related to `subj` of relationship as defined by `rel_type` into `cls` and then further returns the `cls` object.

- `Store.load_indexed(index_name, key,value, cls)`: It queries the legacy index, loads all the nodes that are mapped by key-value, and returns the associated object.

- `Store.relate(subj, rel_type, obj, properties=None)`: It defines the relationship between two nodes, where `subj` and `cls` are two nodes connected by `rel_type`. By default, all relationships point towards the right node.

- `Store.save(subj, node=None)`: It save and creates a given entity/node – `subj` into the graph database. The second argument is of type `Node`, which if given will not create a new node and will change the already existing node.

- `Store.save_indexed(index_name,key,value,subj)`: It saves the given entity into the graph and also creates an entry into the given index for future reference.

Refer to `http://py2neo.org/2.0/ext/ogm.html#py2neo.ext.ogm.Store` for the complete list of methods exposed by `Store` class.

Let's move on to the next section where we will use the OGM for mutating our social network data model.

 OGM supports Neo4j version 1.9, so all features of Neo4j 2.0 and above are not supported such as labels.

Social network application with Flask-RESTful and OGM

In this section, we will develop a full-fledged application for mutating our social network data and will also talk about the basics of Flask-RESTful and OGM.

Creating object model

Perform the following steps to create the object model and CRUD/search functions for our social network data:

1. Our social network data contains two kind of entities — Person and Movies. So as a first step let's create a package `model` and within the `model` package let's define a module `SocialDataModel.py` with two classes — `Person` and `Movie`:

```
class Person(object):
    def __init__(self, name=None,surname=None,age=None,country=No
ne):
        self.name=name
        self.surname=surname
        self.age=age
        self.country=country


class Movie(object):
    def __init__(self, movieName=None):
        self.movieName=movieName
```

2. Next, let's define another package `operations` and two python modules `ExecuteCRUDOperations.py` and `ExecuteSearchOperations.py`.

3. The `ExecuteCRUDOperations` module will contain the following three classes:

    ○ `DeleteNodesRelationships`: It will contain one method each for deleting `People` nodes and `Movie` nodes and in the `__init__` method, we will establish the connection to the graph database.

```
class DeleteNodesRelationships(object):
    '''
    Define the Delete Operation on Nodes
    '''
    def __init__(self,host,port,username,password):
        #Authenticate and Connect to the Neo4j Graph Database
        py2neo.authenticate(host+':'+port, username,
password)
        graph = Graph('http://'+host+':'+port+'/db/data/')
```

```
store = Store(graph)
#Store the reference of Graph and Store.
self.graph=graph
self.store=store

    def deletePersonNode(self,node):
        #Load the node from the Neo4j Legacy Index
cls = self.store.load_indexed('personIndex', 'name', node.
name, Person)
        #Invoke delete method of store class
        self.store.delete(cls[0])

    def deleteMovieNode(self,node):
        #Load the node from the Neo4j Legacy Index
  cls = self.store.load_indexed('movieIndex',    'name',node.
movieName, Movie)
        #Invoke delete method of store class
            self.store.delete(cls[0])
```

> Deleting nodes will also delete the associated relationships, so there is no need to have functions for deleting relationships. Nodes without any relationship do not make much sense for many business use cases, especially in a social network, unless there is a specific need or an exceptional scenario.

° UpdateNodesRelationships: It will contain one method each for updating People nodes and Movie nodes and, in the __init__ method, we will establish the connection to the graph database.

```
class UpdateNodesRelationships(object):
    '''
    Define the Update Operation on Nodes
    '''

    def __init__(self,host,port,username,password):
        #Write code for connecting to server

    def updatePersonNode(self,oldNode,newNode):
        #Get the old node from the Index
        cls = self.store.load_indexed('personIndex', 'name',
oldNode.name, Person)
        #Copy the new values to the Old Node
        cls[0].name=newNode.name
        cls[0].surname=newNode.surname
```

```
            cls[0].age=newNode.age
            cls[0].country=newNode.country
            #Delete the Old Node form Index
            self.store.delete(cls[0])
            #Persist the updated values again in the Index
            self.store.save_unique('personIndex', 'name',
        newNode.name, cls[0])

        def updateMovieNode(self,oldNode,newNode):
             #Get the old node from the Index
            cls = self.store.load_indexed('movieIndex', 'name',
        oldNode.movieName, Movie)
            #Copy the new values to the Old Node
            cls[0].movieName=newNode.movieName
            #Delete the Old Node form Index
            self.store.delete(cls[0])
            #Persist the updated values again in the Index
            self.store.save_ unique('personIndex', 'name',
        newNode.name, cls[0])
```

○ CreateNodesRelationships: This class will contain methods for creating People and Movies nodes and relationships and will then further persist them to the database. As with the other classes/ module, it will establish the connection to the graph database in the __init__ method:

```
class CreateNodesRelationships(object):
    '''
    Define the Create Operation on Nodes
    '''
    def __init__(self,host,port,username,password):
        #Write code for connecting to server
    '''
    Create a person and store it in the Person Dictionary.
    Node is not saved unless save() method is invoked.
Helpful in bulk creation
    '''
    def createPerson(self,name,surName=None,age=None,country
=None):
        person = Person(name,surName,age,country)
        return person


    '''
    Create a movie and store it in the Movie Dictionary.
```

```
        Node is not saved unless save() method is invoked.
Helpful in bulk creation
    '''
    def createMovie(self,movieName):
        movie = Movie(movieName)
        return movie


    '''
    Create a relationships between 2 nodes and invoke a local
method of Store class.
    Relationship is not saved unless Node is saved or save()
method is invoked.
    '''
    def createFriendRelationship(self,startPerson,endPerson):
        self.store.relate(startPerson, 'FRIEND', endPerson)


    '''
    Create a TEACHES relationships between 2 nodes and invoke
a local method of Store class.
    Relationship is not saved unless Node is saved or save()
method is invoked.
    '''
    def createTeachesRelationship(self,startPerson,endPers
on):
        self.store.relate(startPerson, 'TEACHES', endPerson)
    '''
    Create a HAS_RATED relationships between 2 nodes and
invoke a local method of Store class.
    Relationship is not saved unless Node is saved or save()
method is invoked.
    '''
    def createHasRatedRelationship(self,startPerson,movie,ra
tings):
        self.store.relate(startPerson, 'HAS_RATED',
movie,{'ratings':ratings})
    '''
    Based on type of Entity Save it into the Server/ database
    '''
    def save(self,entity,node):
        if(entity=='person'):
            self.store.save_unique('personIndex', 'name',
node.name, node)
        else:
            self.store.save_unique('movieIndex','name',node.
movieName,node)
```

Next we will define other Python module operations, `ExecuteSearchOperations.py`. This module will define two classes, each containing one method for searching `Person` and `Movie` node and of-course the `__init__` method for establishing a connection with the server:

```
class SearchPerson(object):
    '''
    Class for Searching and retrieving the the People Node from
server
    '''

    def __init__(self,host,port,username,password):
        #Write code for connecting to server

    def searchPerson(self,personName):
        cls = self.store.load_indexed('personIndex',
'name', personName, Person)
        return cls;

class SearchMovie(object):
    '''
    Class for Searching and retrieving the the Movie Node from
server
    '''
    def __init__(self,host,port,username,password):
        #Write code for connecting to server

    def searchMovie(self,movieName):
        cls = self.store.load_indexed('movieIndex', 'name',
movieName, Movie)
        return cls;
```

We are done with our data model and the utility classes that will perform the CRUD and search operation over our social network data using py2neo OGM.

Now let's move on to the next section and develop some REST services over our data model.

Creating REST APIs over data models

In this section, we will create and expose REST services for mutating and searching our social network data using the data model created in the previous section.

In our social network data model, there will be operations on either the `Person` or `Movie` nodes, and there will be one more operation which will define the relationship between `Person` and `Person` or `Person` and `Movie`.

So let's create another package `service` and define another module `MutateSocialNetworkDataService.py`. In this module, apart from regular imports from `flask` and `flask_restful`, we will also import classes from our custom packages created in the previous section and create objects of model classes for performing CRUD and search operations. Next we will define the different classes or services which will define the structure of our REST Services.

The `PersonService` class will define the GET, POST, PUT, and DELETE operations for searching, creating, updating, and deleting the `Person` nodes.

```
class PersonService(Resource):
    '''
    Defines operations with respect to Entity - Person
    '''
    #example - GET http://localhost:5000/person/Bradley
    def get(self, name):
        node = searchPerson.searchPerson(name)
        #Convert into JSON and return it back
        return jsonify(name=node[0].name,surName=node[0].
surname,age=node[0].age,country=node[0].country)


    #POST http://localhost:5000/person
    #{"name": "Bradley","surname": "Green","age":
"24","country": "US"}
    def post(self):

        jsonData = request.get_json(cache=False)
        attr={}
        for key in jsonData:
            attr[key]=jsonData[key]
            print(key,' = ',jsonData[key] )
        person = createOperation.
createPerson(attr['name'],attr['surname'],attr['age'],attr['country'])
        createOperation.save('person',person)

        return jsonify(result='success')
    #POST http://localhost:5000/person/Bradley
    #{"name": "Bradley1","surname": "Green","age": "24","country":
"US"}
    def put(self,name):
        oldNode = searchPerson.searchPerson(name)
```

```
        jsonData = request.get_json(cache=False)
        attr={}
        for key in jsonData:
            attr[key] = jsonData[key]
            print(key,' = ',jsonData[key] )
        newNode = Person(attr['name'],attr['surname'],attr['age'],att
r['country'])

        updateOperation.updatePersonNode(oldNode[0],newNode)

        return jsonify(result='success')

    #DELETE http://localhost:5000/person/Bradley1
    def delete(self,name):
        node = searchPerson.searchPerson(name)
        deleteOperation.deletePersonNode(node[0])
        return jsonify(result='success')
```

The MovieService class will define the GET, POST, and DELETE operations for searching, creating, and deleting the Movie nodes. This service will not support the modification of Movie nodes because, once the Movie node is defined, it does not change in our data model. Movie service is similar to our Person service and leverages our data model for performing various operations.

The RelationshipService class only defines POST which will create the relationship between the person and other given entity and can either be another Person or Movie. Following is the structure of the POST method:

```
    '''
        Assuming that the given nodes are already created this operation
        will associate Person Node either with another Person or Movie
    Node.

        Request for Defining relationship between 2 persons: -
            POST http://localhost:5000/relationship/person/Bradley
            {"entity_type":"person","person.
    name":"Matthew","relationship": "FRIEND"}
        Request for Defining relationship between Person and Movie
            POST http://localhost:5000/relationship/person/Bradley
            {"entity_type":"Movie","movie.movieName":"Avengers",'relations
    hip": "HAS_RATED"
            "relationship.ratings":"4"}
    '''

    def post(self, entity,name):
        jsonData = request.get_json(cache=False)
```

```
        attr={}
        for key in jsonData:
            attr[key]=jsonData[key]
            print(key,' = ',jsonData[key] )


        if(entity == 'person'):
            startNode = searchPerson.searchPerson(name)
            if(attr['entity_type']=='movie'):
                endNode = searchMovie.searchMovie(attr['movie.
movieName'])
                createOperation.createHasRatedRelationship(startNo
de[0], endNode[0], attr['relationship.ratings'])
                createOperation.save('person', startNode[0])
            elif (attr['entity_type']=='person' and attr['relationship
']=='FRIEND'):
                endNode = searchPerson.searchPerson(attr['person.
name'])
                createOperation.createFriendRelationship(startNode[0],
endNode[0])
                createOperation.save('person', startNode[0])
            elif (attr['entity_type']=='person' and attr['relationship
']=='TEACHES'):
                endNode = searchPerson.searchPerson(attr['person.
name'])
                createOperation.createTeachesRelationship(startNo
de[0], endNode[0])
                createOperation.save('person', startNode[0])
        else:
            raise HTTPException("Value is not Valid")


        return jsonify(result='success')
```

At the end, we will define our __main__ method, which will bind our services with
the specific URLs and bring up our application:

```
if __name__ == '__main__':
    api.add_resource(PersonService,'/person','/person/<string:name>')
    api.add_resource(MovieService,'/movie','/
movie/<string:movieName>')
    api.add_resource(RelationshipService,'/relationship','/relationshi
p/<string:entity>/<string:name>')
    webapp.run(debug=True)
```

And we are done!!! Execute our `MutateSocialNetworkDataService.py` as a regular Python module and your REST-based services are up and running. Users of this app can use any REST-based clients such as SOAP-UI and can execute the various REST services for performing CRUD and search operations.

 Follow the comments provided in the code samples for the format of the request/response.

In this section, we created and exposed REST-based services using Flask, Flask-RESTful, and OGM and performed CRUD and search operations over our social network data model.

Summary

In this chapter, we learned about creating web-based applications using Flask. We also used Flasks extensions such as Flask-RESTful for creating/exposing REST APIs for data manipulation. Finally, we created a full blown REST-based application over our social network data using Flask, Flask-RESTful, and py2neo OGM.

In the next chapter, we will discuss in detail about the integration of Django and Neo4j.

6
Using Neo4j with Django and Neomodel

Web frameworks or web application frameworks are the standard, structured, and faster way of developing web-based applications that can be exposed over the Internet to a wide variety of users.

Django (`https://www.djangoproject.com/`) is one of the powerful web-based frameworks written in Python for rapidly creating Python-based web-enabled applications in minutes.

Though there are many other Python web-based frameworks, Django is one of the obvious choices for creating enterprise-grade and large-scale systems. Based on MVC pattern, Django is fast, secure, and scalable.

Django follows the "batteries included" philosophy of Python (`https://docs.python.org/2/tutorial/stdlib.html#batteries-included`), where it provides various tools and utilities such as templating, forms, routing, authentication, basic database administration, and so on, which makes it easy for the developers to dive in and develop web applications in the shortest possible time.

On the other hand, Neomodel (`https://github.com/robinedwards/neomodel`) is the **Object Graph Mapper** (**OGM**) framework for Neo4j that is built on py2neo and provides the Django model style definition. It provides a powerful query API, along with transactions and hooks for Django signals (`https://docs.djangoproject.com/en/1.7/topics/signals/`).

In the last chapter, we discussed about Flask for building RESTful APIs. In this chapter, we will learn to develop and integrate the Python-based web framework Django with Neomodel for building web-based applications over Neo4j.

This chapter will cover the following points:

- Installing and configuring Neomodel
- Declaring models and properties
- Adding relationships to models
- Running Cypher queries
- Using Neomodel in a Django app

Installing and configuring Neomodel

In this section, we will talk about installing and configuring Neomodel on a virtual environment provided by Python.

Py2neo provides the lower-level APIs for interacting with Neo4j, which sometimes becomes difficult as a lot of boilerplate code needs to be written for performing CRUD or search operation over Neo4j database. Though it provides APIs for dealing with all the features of Neo4j version 1.9 or earlier, fundamentally it doesn't provide object relational mapping between the entities or nodes. In contrast, Neomodel exploits the same py2neo APIs and adds some more code to support the features of Neo4j 2.0 and above, such as labels, constraints, and so on, and provides object relational mapping for Neo4j entities or nodes. We will discuss this in detail in the upcoming sections but let's first look at the basic steps of installing Neomodel.

Neomodel is available in PyPI (`https://pypi.python.org/pypi/neomodel`), so it can be installed using the `pip` command. However, the latest version of Neomodel, version 1.0.2, is developed upon py2neo 1.6.4, so if you have already installed py2neo 2.0.5 then installing Neomodel will downgrade your py2neo version to 1.6.4, which will introduce lot of changes in the code which was specifically written for py2neo 2.0.5.

In order to avoid that, we will install Virtual Environment for working with Neomodel, which will be totally separate from our original Python environment, and we can have different versions of the same software in the same machine.

Perform the following steps to install Virtual Environment on Windows:

1. Open the console or command prompt and use pip to install Virtual Environment from Python Repository PyPi for Windows:

   ```
   pip install virtualenvwrapper-win
   ```

2. The command in step 1 will download, install, and configure the Virtual Environment utility `virtualenvwrapper-win` from the Python repository.

3. Next, on the same console, define a system environment variable WORKON_HOME, which will define the location where all your virtual environments and their associated configurations will be saved:

```
set WORKON_HOME= <location of directory>
```

4. On the same console, create a virtual environment by executing the following command:

```
mkvirtualenv CH-6-Neomodel
```

5. After successful completion of the previous command, your virtual environment is created and you are also switched to this new environment, which is named as CH-6-Neomodel.

   This new environment is a raw environment and does not contain any Python extensions which we installed while working on examples from earlier chapters.

6. Next, we will execute the following command in our new virtual environment and install Neomodel:

```
pip install Neomodel
```

7. After successful completion of the preceding command, you can also execute pip list which will produce the results similar to the following screenshot:

```
(CH-6-Neomodel) C:\>pip install neomodel
Collecting neomodel
  Downloading neomodel-1.0.2.tar.gz
Collecting py2neo==1.6.4 (from neomodel)
  Downloading py2neo-1.6.4.tar.gz (217kB)
    100% |################################| 221kB 524kB/s
Collecting pytz==2014.7 (from neomodel)
  Downloading pytz-2014.7.tar.bz2 (166kB)
    100% |################################| 167kB 655kB/s
Installing collected packages: pytz, py2neo, neomodel
  Running setup.py install for pytz
  Running setup.py install for py2neo
    building 'py2neo.packages.jsonstream.cjsonstream' extension
  Running setup.py install for neomodel
Successfully installed neomodel-1.0.2 py2neo-1.6.4 pytz-2014.7

(CH-6-Neomodel) C:\>pip list
neomodel (1.0.2)
pip (6.0.8)
py2neo (1.6.4)
pytz (2014.7)
setuptools (12.0.5)

(CH-6-Neomodel) C:\>_
```

And we are done!!! Our Neomodel is installed and no more configurations are required.

Examples in the subsequent sections will be executed in the same virtual environment. If you closed your console, you can always open a new console and execute `workon CH-6-Neomodel` to again move to your virtual environment.

 Refer to `https://pypi.python.org/pypi/ virtualenvwrapper-win` for other convenient commands available for working with Virtual Environments.

Declaring models and properties

In this section, we will discuss creating the model and the properties using various APIs exposed by Neomodel. We will also learn about the mapping of the models and properties with Neo4j nodes.

Let's move forward and see how Neomodel provides the mapping of Neo4j nodes and creates a data model.

Neo4j consists of nodes and these nodes can further have labels and properties. Properties in Neo4j can contain String, Numeric, Boolean, or collections of any other type of value. Refer to `http://neo4j.com/docs/stable/property-values- detailed.html` for the complete list of data types supported by Neo4j.

Neomodel defines all the necessary base classes for mapping Neo4j nodes and properties, provides a wrapper over the structure of Neo4j, and provides the full-fledged functionality of an object graph mapping.

Defining nodes

Neomodel defines `neomodel.StructuredNode` as a base class that needs to be extended by all the user defined classes, which intend to define the structure of a node and further the name the class will be saved as the label for that particular node.

For example, in our social networking data model, we have three types of nodes—Male, Female, and Movie. So we need to define three different classes for each type of node with the same name as their label names. Let's define a Python module by the name of `Model.py` and within that define the three classes:

```
from neomodel import (StructuredNode)

class Male(StructuredNode):
    print('Class for Male Nodes')
```

```
class Female(StructuredNode):
    print('Class for Female Nodes')

class Movie(StructuredNode):
    print('Class for Movie Nodes')
```

Next, we will enhance our data model and define the properties for each of the nodes.

Defining properties

Neomodel defines `neomodel.Property` as the base class that is extended by the following classes, providing the mapping between Python and Neo4j property data types:

- `neomodel.StringProperty`: This defines a sequence of Unicode characters, which is equivalent to the Python `String`.

- `neomodel.IntegerProperty`: This defines an Integer, which is equivalent to the Python `int` (`signed Integer`).

- `neomodel.FloatProperty`: This holds a floating point value, which is equivalent to `float` in Python.

- `neomodel.BooleanProperty`: This defines a Boolean which can be either `True` or `False` and is equivalent to the Python `bool`.

- `neomodel.ArraryProperty`: This defines an array of value, which is equivalent to `list` in Python.

- `neomodel.DateProperty`: This leverages the Python `datetime.date` class and holds the date.

- `neomodel.DateTimeProperty`: This is an extension of `neomodel.DateProperty` which contains time along with the date.

- `neomodel.JSONProperty`: This is a special type of property that holds a String in JSON format. It leverages the Python JSON module for marshalling and un-marshalling the Strings. Refer to `https://docs.python.org/3/library/json.html` for more information on handling JSON in Python.

- `neomodel.AliasProperty`: This is another special type of property that can be used to define the aliases to the properties of the given model and can be further used in the same fashion as the original properties.

While we define or work with these properties, we can also define certain validations or integrity constraints on each of these properties:

- `unique_index`: This is a Boolean value and if defined then a unique constraint is created on that property, which is equivalent to unique constraints defined by Neo4j (`http://neo4j.com/docs/stable/query-constraints.html`).

- `index`: This is a Boolean value that defines whether the property needs to be indexed or not. This helps in faster searching by creating an index in Neo4j on the given property (`http://neo4j.com/docs/stable/query-schema-index.html`).

- `required`: This is a Boolean value stating whether the value is required or if it can be `Null`.

- `Default`: It defines the default value of the property in case the user does not provide any value.

Let's enhance our data model and define the properties in our classes `Male`, `Female`, and `Movie`, which would look something like the following:

```
from neomodel import (StructuredNode, StringProperty, IntegerProperty)

class Male(StructuredNode):
    print('Class for Male Nodes')
    #Names should not be Duplicate, so we define it as required
    #and instruct to create a Unique_Index
    name = StringProperty(unique_index=True, required=True)
    surname = StringProperty()
    age = IntegerProperty()
    country = StringProperty(default='US')

class Female(StructuredNode):
    print('Class for Male Female Nodes')
    #Names should not be Duplicate, so we define it as required
    #and instruct to create a Unique_Index
    name = StringProperty(unique_index=True, required=True)
    surname = StringProperty()
    age = IntegerProperty()
    country = StringProperty(default='US')
    ratings = RelationshipTo('Movie', 'HAS_RATED', OneOrMore)

class Movie(StructuredNode):
    print('Class for Movie Nodes')
```

```
#Movie Names should not be Duplicate, so we define it as required
#and instruct to create a Unique_Index
movieName = StringProperty(unique_index=True, required=True)
```

And we are done !!!

We have defined the nodes, properties, and integrity constraints that will be part of our social data model. Now we have to define the relationships in our data model.

But before that, let's see the various methods exposed by Neomodel for persisting our data model and other useful methods for querying it.

Persisting and querying a social data model

In this section, we will discuss persisting and querying our social data model using APIs exposed by Neomodel.

Nodes and relationships are the basic entities defined in the graphs and all the other features, whether querying, saving, deleting, or updating, revolve around these two entities only. Neomodel follows the same concept and provides some useful methods in `neomodel.StructuredNode` for performing various CRUD and search operations.

Let's discuss a few of the useful methods and the rest we will discuss in the upcoming sections.

- `nodes()`: This method is used to provide the object of `NodeSet` defined in Python module `Match.py` (`https://github.com/robinedwards/neomodel/blob/1.0.2/neomodel/match.py`). The `NodeSet` class provides access to the traversals that are used to traverse the graph and search the specific type of nodes based on the filtering criteria provided by the user.

- `__eq__(node)`: This returns `true` if the given node and the node invoking this method are equal, else `false`.

- `__ne__(node)`: This returns `false` if the given node and the node invoking this method are equal, else `true`.

- `labels()`: This returns the object of dictionary containing the labels associated with the node.

- `save()`: This persists the node in the Neo4j database.

- `delete()`: This deletes the node from the Neo4j database.

- `refresh()`: This reloads or refreshes all properties of the node from the Neo4j database.

- `cypher(query, params=None)`: This executes a given Cypher query and returns the results.

The __eq__ and __ne__ methods are special methods that provide the == and != functionality for objects. They are not really meant to be called directly (hence the obscure name).

Now, using the preceding methods, let's create and persist our social data model and then finally query/search the Neo4j database.

Perform the following steps for creating the model:

1. Open your Neo4jshell and execute the following Cypher queries to delete any existing data from your Neo4j database:

   ```
   MATCH (n)-[r]-(n1) delete n,r,n1;
   MATCH (n) delete n;
   ```

2. Next, define a new module ExploreSocialDataModel.py and, within this module, define class CreateDataModel().

3. Define a new function createNodes() within CreateDataModel(), which will contain the code snippet for creating nodes.

4. Next, create objects of Male, Female, or Movie and define the values of the properties. Finally invoke the save() method on each of the Male, Female, or Movie objects.

   ```
   def createNodes(self):
   try:
   #Creating Males
   Male(name='Bradley',surname='Green',age=24,country='US').save()
   Male(name='Matthew',surname='Cooper',age=36,country='US').save()
   Male(name='John',surname='Goodman',age=24,country='Mexico').save()
   Male(name='Ripley',surname='Aniston',country='US').save()
   #Creating FeMales
   Female(name='Lisa',surname='Adams',age=15,country='Canada').save()
   Female(name='Annie',surname='Behr',age=24,country='Canada').save()
   #Creating Movies
   Movie(movieName='First Blood').save()
   Movie(movieName='Avengers').save()
   Movie(movieName='Matrix').save()

       except UniqueProperty:
           #Quietly move on as the Nodes already exists.
           Pass
   ```

5. Refer to the *Creating a social network with py2neo* section of *Chapter 4, Getting Python and Neo4j to Talk Py2neo,* for more details on the structure of social data model.

6. Next, from your main method, invoke `createNodes()` and run your code on the console by executing `python ExploreSocialDataModel.py`.

And we are done!

All our nodes are created and persisted in the Neo4j database. We will talk about defining the relationship in the next section, but before that, let's look at how to retrieve or search data using Neomodel APIs.

Let's define two utility methods in `ExploreSocialDataModel.py` to search and retrieve the data back from the database:

- `searchNodebyUniqueName(name)`: This method will search all types of nodes within our database and see whether the name attribute of the nodes matches the value provided by the user. It will use the `nodes()` method of the `StructuredNode` class to search and provide the results back to the user. The structure of this method will be as shown in the following code snippet:

```
def searchNodebyUniqueName(name):
    try:
        print('Searching for Nodes with Name = ',name)
        #Search all Nodes tagged with Label Male
        node = Male.nodes.get(name=name)
        #if found, Print all its attributes
        print(node.labels(),': Name=',node.name,', Surname=',node.
surname,', Age=',node.age,', Country=',node.country)
        #No need to process further code and return back from
lthere itself.
        return node
    #DoesNotExist Exception is raised in case nothing is found
    except DoesNotExist:
        pass
    try:
        #Search all Nodes tagged with Label Female
        node = Female.nodes.get(name=name)
        print(node.labels(),': Name=',node.name,', Surname=',node.
surname,', Age=',node.age,', Country=',node.country)
        return node
    #DoesNotExist Exception is raised in case nothing is found
    except DoesNotExist:
        pass
```

```
try:
    #Search all Nodes tagged with Label Movie
    node = Movie.nodes.get(movieName=name)
    print(node.labels(),': MovieName=',node.movieName)
    return node
#DoesNotExist Exception is raised in case nothing is found
except DoesNotExist:
    pass
#if it reaches here that means no Nodes exists by the Given
Name
    print('Sorry...Nothing Found...try again')
    return
```

We can invoke this method directly from our main method, for example `searchNodebyUniqueName('Bradley')`.

- `def filterMalesByAge(age,criteria):` This method searches nodes tagged with the label `Male`, based on the provided arguments `age` and `criteria`, which can be either `less`, `more`, or `equal`. This method utilizes the `NodeSet.filter(...)` for filtering the nodes. Filters in `NodeSet` define the same Django-style filter formats, where you can use the properties with a double underscore suffixed with operators.

```
def filterMalesByAge(age,criteria):

    if(criteria=='more'):
        print('Searching for Males where Age >',age)
        nodes = Male.nodes.filter(age__gt=age)
        for n in nodes:
            print('Name=',n.name,', Surname=',n.surname,',
Age=',n.age,', Country=',n.country)
        return nodes
    elif(criteria=='less'):
        print('Searching for Males where age <',age)
        nodes = Male.nodes.filter(age__lt=age)
        for n in nodes:
            print('Name=',n.name,', Surname=',n.surname,',
Age=',n.age,', Country=',n.country)
        return nodes
    else:
        print('Searching for exact Match where Age = ',age)
        nodes = Male.nodes.filter(age=age)
        for n in nodes:
            print('Name=',n.name,', Surname=',n.surname,',
Age=',n.age,', Country=',n.country)
        return nodes
```

We can invoke this method also from our main method, but with different criteria:

```
filterMalesByAge(1,'more')
filterMalesByAge(50,'less')
filterMalesByAge(25,'equal')
```

Apart from the filters specified in the preceding piece of code, we can also use the following filters:

- ○ lte: For filtering values which are less than or equal to the given criteria
- ○ gte: For filtering values which are greater than or equal to the given criteria
- ○ ne: For filtering values which are not equal to the given criteria

Filtering can be applied to any of the properties of the node or relationship.

In this section, we discussed about the various APIs exposed by Neomodel for creating nodes and their associated properties and further discussed the powerful search APIs for searching and retrieving the results from the database.

Let's move on to the next section and discuss the process of creating relationships in Neomodel. We will enhance our data model and create relationship between males, females, and movies.

Adding relationships to models

Neomodel provides the following classes in the neomodel package for defining relationships between nodes or entities:

- Relationship: This class is used to define a bi-directional relationship in which the "direction" of the relationship does not matter. It can be in any direction. For example, in our social data model we are using the FRIEND relationship in which direction does not matter, because if one person declares being a friend to another then vice-versa is also true.

- RelationshipTo: It is used to define the outgoing relationship.

- RelationshipFrom: It is used to define the incoming relationship.

All of these classes accept four parameters and expose the `connect()` method to establish a relationship with the given node. The following is the explanation of each parameter required by the relationship classes:

- **Class name**: This is the name of the class that enjoys the relationship with the class in which the relationship is defined.
- **Relationship type**: This is the type or name of the relationship.
- **Cardinality**: It defines the number of incoming or outgoing relationships for a given entity. It defines three classes to define the cardinality — `ZeroOrMore`, `OneOrMore`, and `One`. It raises the `CardinalityViolation` exception if the constraints imposed by cardinality are violated.
- **Model**: This is used to define the properties of the relationship and should be an instance of `StructuredRel`.

Now let's move on and enhance our social data model `Model.py` and define relationships. Our model contains the following three types of relationships:

- `FRIEND`: As we discussed earlier, direction does not matter, so we will create an object of `Relationship` and define an attribute to hold the relationship in `Male` and `Female` domain classes. We need to define two relationship objects for each Male and Female, because two males or two females or both a male and a female can be friends:

```
maleFriends = Relationship('Male', 'FRIEND', OneOrMore)
femaleFriends = Relationship('Female', 'FRIEND', OneOrMore)
```

- `TEACHES`: This relationship defines a student and teacher relationship which does have a direction and, as per our data model, only males are a part of this relationship. So here we will use `RelationshipTo` and define the relationship property in the `Male` domain class:

```
teacher = RelationshipTo('Male', 'TEACHES', OneOrMore)
```

- `HAS_RATED`: This relationship signifies that either a male or a female has rated one movie. So here we will use `RelationshipTo` in both the `Male` and `Female` domain classes. Also, the `HAS_RATED` relationship contains the property that defines a numeric value to signify the rating provided by the male or female. So we have to create another class in `Model.py` that will extend `StructuredRel` and define property of type Integer:

```
class Ratings(StructuredRel):
    ratings = IntegerProperty()
```

The definition of relationship in `Male` and `Female` would be:

```
ratings = RelationshipTo('Movie', 'HAS_RATED', OneOrMore
,model=Ratings)
```

Save your model and we are done with all the modifications to our social data model. Now let's enhance our `CreateDataModel()` class and write code for creating relationships.

Perform the following steps to create the FRIEND, TEACHES, and HAS_RATED relationships between males, females, and movies:

1. Create a new function `createFriendRelationship(self)`.

2. Now, in this function, search the nodes using `searchNodebyUniqueName` and then use the `connect()` method to create a relationship, as follows:

```
def createFriendRelationship(self):
        print('Start creating FRIEND Relationship between given
nodes')
        searchNodebyUniqueName('Bradley').maleFriends.connect(sear
chNodebyUniqueName('Matthew'))
        searchNodebyUniqueName('Bradley').femaleFriends.connect(se
archNodebyUniqueName('Lisa'))
        searchNodebyUniqueName('Matthew').femaleFriends.connect(se
archNodebyUniqueName('Lisa'))
        searchNodebyUniqueName('Lisa').maleFriends.connect(searchN
odebyUniqueName('John'))
        searchNodebyUniqueName('Annie').maleFriends.connect(search
NodebyUniqueName('Ripley'))
        searchNodebyUniqueName('Ripley').femaleFriends.connect(sea
rchNodebyUniqueName('Lisa'))
        print('Finished creating FRIEND Relationship between given
nodes')
```

3. Next, we will create a new function `createTeachesRelationship(self)`, and in this function search the nodes using `searchNodebyUniqueName`, and then use the `connect()` method to create a TEACHES relationship, as follows:

```
def createTeachesRelationship(self):
print('Start creating Student/ Teacher relationship between given
nodes')
searchNodebyUniqueName('Bradley').teacher.connect(searchNodebyUniq
ueName('Matthew'))
print('Finished creating Student/ Teacher relationship between
given nodes')
```

4. Next, we will create a new function `rateMovies(self)`. This function will also search the nodes using `searchNodebyUniqueName` and then use the `connect()` method to create a HAS_RATED relationship, as follows:

```
def rateMovies(self):
        print('Start Rating movies by Males and Females')
        # Search the Movies which needs to be connected
```

```
        firstBlood = searchNodebyUniqueName('First Blood')
        avengers = searchNodebyUniqueName('Avengers')
        #Start Rating Movies
        searchNodebyUniqueName('Bradley').ratings.
connect(firstBlood,{'ratings': '5'})
        searchNodebyUniqueName('Matthew').ratings.connect(firstBlo
od,{'ratings':'4'})
        searchNodebyUniqueName('John').ratings.connect(firstBlood,
{'ratings':'4'})
        searchNodebyUniqueName('Annie').ratings.connect(firstBlood
,{'ratings':'4'})
        searchNodebyUniqueName('Ripley').ratings.connect(firstBloo
d,{'ratings':'4'})
        searchNodebyUniqueName('Lisa').ratings.connect(avengers,{'
ratings':'5'})
        searchNodebyUniqueName('Matthew').ratings.connect(avengers
,{'ratings':'4'})
        searchNodebyUniqueName('Annie').ratings.connect(avengers,{
'ratings':'3'})
        print('Finished Rating of movies by Males and Females')
```

5. Next, we will update our main method and invoke these new functions:

```
if __name__ == '__main__':
    print('Start')
    create = CreateDataModel()
    create.createNodes()
    searchNodebyUniqueName('Bradley')
    filterMalesByAge(1,'more')
    filterMalesByAge(50,'less')
    filterMalesByAge(25,'equal')
    create.createFriendRelationship()
    create.createTeachesRelationship()
    create.rateMovies()
    print('End')
```

And we are done!!!

Now open the console or command prompt and execute `python ExploreSocialDataModel.py`. Your complete data model along with relationships will be created in the Neo4j database.

In this section, we discussed about the process of defining the relationships using Neomodel APIs. Let's move on to the next section and explore the APIs available for executing Cypher queries.

Running Cypher queries

In this section, we will talk about executing the raw Cypher queries to handle complex requirements and then further converting them into a model and presenting it to the end user.

Cypher queries can be executed by the following two ways:

- Using the `StructuredNode.cypher(query,params)` function
- Using the `neomodel.db.cypher_query(query, params)` function

In the first option, the query definition needs to be defined within the domain class itself and then it uses `StructuredNode.inflate()` for creating domain objects from the raw Cypher results.

For example, let's assume that we need to retrieve and print all the male friends of a given node. So we will modify our `Model.py` and add the following method in the `Male` class:

```
def getAllMaleFriends(self):
        print('printing All Male friends')
        query = 'START a=node({self}) MATCH (a)-[:FRIEND]-(b:Male)
RETURN b'
        results, columns = self.cypher(query)
        #Declare a List and then populate it with results
        maleList = []
            for row in results:
                maleList.append(self.inflate(row[0]))
        return maleList
```

Next, in our `ExploreSocialDataModel.py`, let's define the following method and invoke it from our `main` method:

```
def maleFriendsUsingModel():
        male = searchNodebyUniqueName('Bradley')
        people = male.getAllMaleFriends()

        for male in people:
            print(male.name)
```

Now, let's define a new function `maleFriends()` which does the same thing but outside our data model; that is, directly in our `ExploreSocialDataModel.py`:

```
def maleFriends():

        query = 'MATCH (a:Male{name: {n0_name}})-[:FRIEND]-(b:Male)
RETURN b'
        results, columns = db.cypher_query(query,{'n0_
name':'Bradley'})
        for row in results:
            male = Male.inflate(row[0])
            print(male.name)
```

Next step is to invoke these methods from the main and you will see that the Cypher queries will print the results on the console.

In this section, we discussed about the APIs and the options available for fulfilling complex requirements by executing raw Cypher queries and then converting them back into a model.

Let's move to the next section where we will talk about the integration of Django Web frameworks with Neomodel.

Using Neomodel in a Django app

In this section, we will talk about the integration of Django and Neomodel.

Django is a Python-based, powerful, robust, and scalable web-based application development framework. It is developed upon the **Model-View-Controller (MVC)** design pattern where developers can design and develop a scalable enterprise-grade application within no time.

We will not go into the details of Django as a web-based framework but will assume that the readers have a basic understanding of Django and some hands-on experience in developing web-based and database-driven applications.

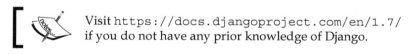 Visit `https://docs.djangoproject.com/en/1.7/` if you do not have any prior knowledge of Django.

Django provides various signals or triggers that are activated and used to invoke or execute some user-defined functions on a particular event.

The framework invokes various signals or triggers if there are any modifications requested to the underlying application data model such as `pre_save()`, `post_save()`, `pre_delete`, `post_delete`, and a few more.

All the functions starting with `pre_` are executed before the requested modifications are applied to the data model, and functions starting with `post_` are triggered after the modifications are applied to the data model. And that's where we will hook our Neomodel framework, where we will capture these events and invoke our custom methods to make similar changes to our Neo4j database.

We can reuse our social data model and the functions defined in `ExploreSocialDataModel.CreateDataModel`.

We only need to register our event and things will be automatically handled by the Django framework. For example, you can register for the event in your Django model (`models.py`) by defining the following statement:

```
signals.pre_save.connect(preSave, sender=Male)
```

In the previous statement, `preSave` is the custom or user-defined method, declared in `models.py`. It will be invoked before any changes are committed to entity `Male`, which is controlled by the Django framework and is different from our Neomodel entity.

Next, in `preSave` you need to define the invocations to the Neomodel entities and save them.

 Refer to the documentation at `https://docs.djangoproject.com/en/1.7/topics/signals/` for more information on implementing signals in Django.

Signals in Neomodel

Neomodel also provides signals that are similar to Django signals and have the same behavior. Neomodel provides the following signals: `pre_save`, `post_save`, `pre_delete`, `post_delete`, and `post_create`.

Neomodel exposes the following two different approaches for implementing signals:

- Define the `pre..()` and `post..()` methods in your model itself and Neomodel will automatically invoke it. For example, in our social data model, we can define `def pre_save(self)` in our `Model.Male` class to receive all events before entities are persisted in the database or server.

- Another approach is using Django-style signals, where we can define the `connect()` method in our Neomodel `Model.py` and it will produce the same results as in Django-based models:

```
signals.pre_save.connect(preSave, sender=Male)
```

 Refer to `http://neomodel.readthedocs.org/en/latest/hooks.html` for more information on signals in Neomodel.

In this section, we discussed about the integration of Django with Neomodel using Django signals. We also talked about the signals provided by Neomodel and their implementation approach.

Summary

In this chapter, we learned about Neomodel and its various features and APIs provided to work with Neo4j. We also discussed about the integration of Neomodel with the Django framework.

In the next chapter, we will discuss in detail about the various aspects, considerations, and decisions for deploying Neo4j in production.

7
Deploying Neo4j in Production

Eventually every software needs to be deployed in production and that's where the real challenge is!

Deciding upon the deployment strategy for any system requires a careful consideration of various factors, such as scalability (number of users now and in future), **Service Level Agreements (SLAs)**, fault tolerance, monitoring, backup, recovery, and many more. All these factors are also known as **Non-Functional Requirements (NFRs)**.

Though many of these factors can be incorporated in the deployment strategy but the architecture and design of software plays an important role in meeting the NFRs.

For example, you can increase hardware to support the growing number of users but there is a limit to how much computing resources (RAM and CPU) you can add to a single machine, and that's where you think about deploying multiple nodes and forming a cluster (`http://en.wikipedia.org/wiki/Computer_cluster`). But what if your software architecture does not support distributed processing of the transactions?

You may run into issues of data integrity, consistency, or race conditions (`http://en.wikipedia.org/wiki/Race_condition`).

It becomes more complex in enterprises where NFRs such as scalability, performance, high availability, backup, and recovery are implicit and in a few scenarios even take priority over the functional requirements.

In the previous chapters, we have discussed about the various frameworks which can help us in designing functional aspects of our software system, developed over Neo4j. In this chapter, we will learn about the various features of Neo4j that will help us in deploying it to meet the needs of enterprises.

This chapter will cover the following points:

- Neo4j logical architecture
- Neo4j physical architecture
- Monitoring the health of the Neo4j nodes
- Backup and recovery

Neo4j logical architecture

In this section, we will talk about the various layers and the role they perform in the overall architecture of Neo4j.

Neo4j is an open source database written in Java and Scala. It implements generic property graph models and provides full database characteristics, including ACID transaction compliance, cluster support, and runtime failover, making it suitable for using graph data in production scenarios.

The following is the high-level logical architecture of Neo4j:

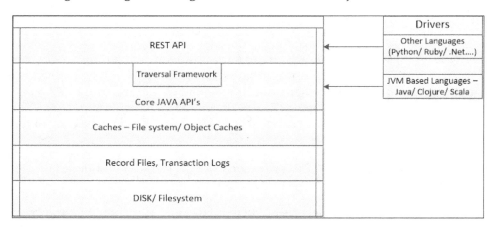

The preceding logical architecture defines the various layers of Neo4j. Let's briefly discuss the role and function of each of these layers.

Disk/filesystem

Neo4j is a fully transactional database that supports all properties of ACID. Thus, we have to ensure that the file system should also support features such as flush (fsync, fdatasync) (`http://en.wikipedia.org/wiki/Sync_(Unix)`), and therefore Neo4j recommends using at least an ext4 filesystem (`http://en.wikipedia.org/wiki/Ext4`), but better would be to use ZFS (`http://en.wikipedia.org/wiki/ZFS`).

 Refer to `https://structr.org/blog/neo4j-performance-on-ext4` for more information on performance improvements on ext4.

Disks play an important role in the overall performance of Neo4j and directly impacts the Read and Write operations.

- **Read operations**: Neo4j uses a threaded read access to the database where queries can be run simultaneously on as many processors as may be available. It recommends to use large memory so that there are far fewer reads from disks for common data, but everything cannot be fitted in memory; thus, in cases where read operations are served by disks, there also it should be reasonably faster. It does not block or lock any read operations; thus, there is no danger of deadlocks in read operations and no need for read transactions.

- **Write operations**: Write operations are really a concern with enterprises needing highly optimized and efficient processes for initial data loads, backup, recovery, and continuous data write operations performed by applications.

Neo4j supports and designs to serve the varied kind of enterprise requirements where it provides transactional and ACID-compliant normal operation for all multithreaded write operations and at the same time a non-transactional low overhead batch inserter for bulk import of large amounts of data. In any case, your write operation will depend upon the I/O capacity of the hardware. Henceforth, the use of fast SSDs (`http://en.wikipedia.org/wiki/Solid-state_drive`) is highly recommended for production environments.

Record files

Neo4j uses various types of files to store nodes, relationships, and properties. All database files are created within the folder on your disks as defined by the property in your neo4j-server.properties `org.neo4j.server.database.location`. All files which start with `neostore.*` contain the actual data about nodes, properties, and relationships.

Let's examine and see the process of data organization and the content of the various database files:

- `neostore.nodestore.*`: This stores information about the nodes. Every node you create is stored here, in a simple, fixed-size record of 9 bytes in total. The first byte is used as a flag. The next four are an integer, that is, the ID of the first relationship of the node. The final four bytes are the integer ID of the first property of the node.

- `neostore.relationshipstore.*`: This stores all the information about the relationships between the nodes in a record of 33 bytes. The first byte signifies the direction, whether this relationship is directed (1) or not (0). Then the next eight bytes are used to define the ID of the two connected nodes (four bytes each). The next four bytes are the ID of the record that represents the type of relationship. The next 16 bytes are used to define the ID of the previous relationship of the first node, the ID of the next relationship of the first node, the ID of the previous relationship of the second node, and finally the ID of the next relationship of the second node. The last four bytes are the ID of the first property of this relationship.

- `neostore.relationshiptypestore.*`: This contains the names of the relationship types. The record size for the type is five bytes. The first is the in-use byte and the last four bytes store the ID of the block that stores the String—name of the relationship type.

- `neostore.propertystore.*`: Properties in Neo4j can be assigned to both nodes and relationships in the key-value format, in which key is the String and value is the Java primitive type or an array of primitive types. Each property record is 25 bytes and starts with the in_use byte. The next four bytes contain the type of property record followed by the next four containing the ID of the property index. The next eight bytes are occupied by a long value containing the ID to a DynamicStore that stores the value or the actual value. Finally there are two integers of four bytes each, which are IDs of the previous and next property of the owning primitive.

- `neostore.propertystore.db.index`: This record starts with an in_use byte, followed by an integer that keeps a property count, and lastly another integer that is the ID in a DynamicStore that keeps the property name, resulting in a total occupancy of 9 bytes.

Node (9 bytes)

inUse	nextRelId	nextPropId

1   5   9

Relationship (33 bytes)

inUse	firstNode	secondNode	relationshipType	firstPrevRelId	firstNextRelId	secondPrevRelId	secondNextRelId	nextPropId

1   5   9   13   17   21   25   29   33

Relationship Type (5 bytes)

inUse	typeBlockId

1   5

Property (33 bytes)

inUse	type	keyIndexId	propBlock	nextPropId

1   3   5   29   33

Property Index (9 bytes)

inUse	propCount	keyBlockId

1   5   9

The previous figure briefly describes the organization of data (in bytes) in the various database files created and maintained by Neo4j.

Transaction logs

Transaction or logical logs in Neo4j are the single source of truth!!!

They maintain a journal of all the events and operations that happen over a Neo4j database, which is helpful in scenarios where the database needs to be recovered from a crash. Logs are rotated on a preconfigured value defined in `neo4j.properties`—`keep_logical_logs`.

Refer to `http://neo4j.com/docs/stable/configuration-logical-logs.html` for more information on transaction logs.

Caches

Caching is one of the most important component in Neo4j and one that directly impacts the read and write performance. Neo4j provides two different types of caching layers. One is file buffer cache and the other is object cache.

File buffer cache uses the off heap memory (OS memory) and directly caches the Neo4j data files stored on disks. All the writes and reads are performed from these caches, which in turn improves the overall throughput. All writes are written to the caches and data in these caches are flushed to durable storage only when the logical logs are rotated. It also improves the write performance by combining many small batches into a single batch that is equivalent to the OS page size.

The following are the properties which help in configuring the size of caches for different Neo4j entities:

Parameter	Default value	Description
`use_memory_mapped_ buffers`	True (except windows)	Enable use of the operating system's memory mapping for storing the file buffer cache windows.
`neostore.nodestore. db.mapped_memory`	25M	Memory required to store the nodes.
`neostore. relationshipstore. db.mapped_memory`	50M	Memory required to store the relationships.
`neostore.propertystore. db.mapped_memory`	90M	Memory required to store the properties of the nodes and relationships.
`neostore.propertystore. db.strings.mapped_memory`	130M	Memory allocated for storing Strings.
`neostore.propertystore. db.arrays.mapped_memory`	130M	Memory allocated for storing arrays.
`mapped_memory_page_size`	1048576	Total size for pages of mapped memory.
`label_block_size`	60 bytes	Block size for storing labels exceeding the in-lined space in node record. This parameter is only considered at the time of store creation, otherwise it is ignored.
`array_block_size`	120 bytes	Block size for storing arrays. This parameter is only considered at the time of store creation, otherwise it is ignored.
`string_block_size`	120 bytes	Block size for storing strings. This parameter is only considered at the time of store creation, otherwise it is ignored.

Object cache stores the actual data (nodes, relationship, and properties) in the form of objects, which further helps in improving the throughput of graph traversals. Unlike file buffer cache, it uses JVM heap space to store the objects. It leverage Java **Garbage Collector (GC)** for cache eviction and uses LRU algorithm.

High performance cache (HPC) is another type of object cache, only available with the enterprise edition of Neo4j. It provides a higher throughput with less memory footprint. It has its own mechanism for cache eviction and does not rely on the garbage collector.

Caching can be configured by modifying the value of `cache_type` in `neo4j.properties`. The following are the possible values of the `cache_type` parameter:

Parameter	Description
None	Do not use any caching.
Soft	Default caching for Neo4j community edition. Provides optimal utilization of memory but may run into GC issues in case of high loads and insufficient memory to hold complete graph in memory.
Weak	Based on the available memory, cached objects are evicted from time to time. Good for large graphs.
Strong	Never evicts or releases the objects from cache. Good for small graphs which can be stored in JVM heap.
Hpc	Only available with Neo4j Enterprise edition and provides a high throughput for reads and writes along with optimal utilization of available memory.

 Refer to `http://neo4j.com/docs/stable/configuration-caches.html` for more details on caching.

Core Java API

Neo4j is written in Java and Scala, and hence it directly exposes certain core APIs that can be directly used by JVM-based languages for working with graphs.

- **Graph database**: The APIs within this category contain various classes for dealing with the basic operations of the graph databases, such as creating database, nodes, labels, and so on. The `org.neo4j.graphdb` package is the base package for all the APIs dealing with the graph operations.

- **Query language** (`org.neo4j.cypher.export`): This contains the classes for executing Cypher queries from the Java code.

- **Graph algorithms** (`org.neo4j.graphalgo`): This defines the classes for invoking various graph algorithms.

- **Management** (org.neo4j.jmx): As the name suggests, it contains JMX APIs for monitoring Neo4j database.

 Enterprise version of Neo4j comes with a new package org.neo4j.management, which is used to provide advanced monitoring.

- **Tooling** (org.neo4j.tooling): This provides classes for performing global operations.

- **Imports** (org.neo4j.unsafe.batchinsert): This contains packages and classes for performing batch imports.

- **Graph matching**: This contains the packages and classes for pattern matching and filtering. It contains two packages—org.neo4j.graphmatching and org.neo4j.graphmatching.filter.

 Enterprise edition provides one more package—org. neo4j.backup—for performing various backups such as online, cold and so on, on the Neo4j database.

Traversal framework

Neo4j provides a callback API for traversing the graph based on certain rules provided by the users. Basically, the users can define an approach to search a graph or subgraph which depends upon certain rules and algorithms such as depth-first or breadth-first.

The following are certain pre-built algorithms that can be used for graph traversals:

- **Shortest path**: Returns algorithm that finds the shortest path between the two given nodes. For more information refer to http://en.wikipedia.org/wiki/Shortest_path_problem.

- **All paths**: Returns algorithm that finds all possible paths between the two given nodes.

- **All simple paths**: Returns algorithm that finds all simple paths of a certain length between the given nodes.

- **Dijkstra**: Returns algorithm that finds the path with lowest cost between two given nodes. For more information, refer to `http://en.wikipedia.org/wiki/Dijkstra's_algorithm`.

- **A***: Returns algorithm that finds the cheapest path between two given nodes. For more information, refer to `http://en.wikipedia.org/wiki/A*_search_algorithm`.

 Refer to `http://neo4j.com/docs/stable/tutorial-traversal-java-api.html` and `http://neo4j.com/docs/stable/rest-api-traverse.html` for more information on the use of traversals with REST.

REST API

Neo4j REST architecture is one of the well-crafted and well-designed architectures. Designed on principles of service discoverability, it exposes the "service root" and from there the users can discover other URIs to perform various CRUD and search operations.

All endpoints are relative to `http://<HOST>:<PORT>/db/data/` which is also known as the "service root" for the other REST end points. You can simply fire the service root using GET operations and it will show its other REST endpoints.

The default representation for all types of request (POST/PUT) and response is JSON.

In order to interact with the JSON interface, the users need to explicitly set the request header as `Accept:application/json` and `Content-Type:application/json`.

 Refer to `http://neo4j.com/docs/stable/rest-api.html` for more information on REST endpoints exposed by Neo4j.

In this section, we discussed logical architectures and various layers of Neo4j, which will help us in understanding and planning our deployments in an efficacious manner. Let's move forward and discuss the physical architecture of Neo4j which is another important aspect of deployment.

Neo4j physical architecture

Neo4j physical architecture, also known as Neo4j HA architecture, provides a robust and scalable architecture and is a fits best for the needs of enterprises.

It mainly provides the following features:

- High availability
- Fault tolerance
- Data replication

Let's discuss the preceding features and also the advanced settings for enabling clustering in Neo4j.

High availability

Neo4j HA architecture provides clustering of Neo4j servers and implements a master-slave architecture.

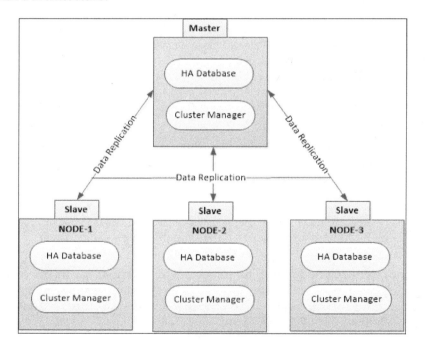

As shown in the previous screenshot, each Neo4j instance has two parts—Neo4j HA database and cluster manager. Neo4j HA database is responsible for storing and retrieving the data, and cluster manager is responsible for ensuring a highly available and fault-tolerant cluster. Neo4j HA database directly communicates to the other instances for data replication with the help of the cluster manager.

The following are the features provided by cluster manager:

- Maintaining and tracking of live and dead nodes
- Enabling of data replication from master node by polling at regular intervals
- Electing master node
- Exposing system health and monitoring via JMX beans

All nodes in a cluster are self-sufficient and any node, either slave or master, can be used for reading data from the database; but all writes have to be persisted or relayed through the master node. Although you can still connect to the slave nodes and relay your write requests but before returning success, they will direct all requests to the master node; only once the master node confirms the success, then only the client will receive a success response. So it is always advisable to relay all writes to the master node while reads can be performed from any node.

Neo4j also provides linear scalability where we can add nodes to the existing cluster and data is asynchronously replicated to the new nodes.

The following configuration is required in `<$NEO4J_HOME>\conf\neo4j-server. properties` for enabling the cluster:

- `org.neo4j.server.database.mode` enables or disables the clustering of Neo4j server. To enable, modify the value to `HA`.

    Refer to *Chapter 1*, *Your First Query with Neo4j* for all other configuration parameters for defining server-IDs and nodes in a cluster.

 Neo4j HA or clustering is only supported in Neo4j Enterprise version.

Fault tolerance

Neo4j provides the custom implementation of multi-paxos paradigm (http://en.wikipedia.org/wiki/Paxos_%28computer_science%29#Multi-Paxos), which provides the following features:

- Cluster management:
    - ○ Tracking of leaving or joining nodes, that is checking the heartbeat of the other participating nodes in a cluster and keeping a track of last sync and its availability
    - ○ Message broadcasting and replication
    - ○ Electing and choosing master node
- Assisting the Neo4j HA database in transaction propagation and data replication

You can also read more about Paxos at http://research.microsoft.com/en-us/um/people/lamport/pubs/paxos-simple.pdf.

Although reads can be served even with a single node, when it comes to writes, it is essential to have a quorum of nodes available in a cluster.

Whenever a Neo4j database instance becomes unavailable, the other database instances in the cluster will detect that and mark it as temporarily failed.

Once the failed instance is available and ready to serve user requests, it is automatically synched up with the other nodes in the cluster.

If the master goes down then another (best-suited) member will be elected and have its role switched from slave to master after a quorum has been reached within the cluster. Writes are blocked during the election process of the master node.

For all those cases where a quorum is not available and we still want to elect a master, Neo4j provides **arbiter nodes**, which can be deployed for achieving the quorum. Arbiter nodes do not contain the data and don't serve the read or write requests. They are used only in the election of the master node with the single purpose of breaking ties.

Arbiter instances are configured in the same way as Neo4j HA members are configured in the conf\neo4j.properties file. The following command is used to start an arbiter instance:

```
<$NEO4J_HOME>\bin\neo4j-arbiter start
```

In cases where the new master performs some changes to the data before the old master recovers, there will be two "branches" of the database after the point where the old master became unavailable. The old master will move away its database (its "branch") and download a full copy from the new master. It will then be marked as available and added as a slave node in the cluster.

Data replication and data locality

Neo4j HA architecture asynchronously replicates the data to other nodes in a cluster. All write operations are first performed by the master node and then the slave nodes are synchronized, or they poll the new data from the last checkpoint from the master node. The behavior of data replication is driven by the following properties, defined in `<$NEO4J_HOME>\conf\neo4j.properties`:

- `ha.pull_interval`: The interval at which slaves will pull updates from the master. Unit is in seconds.

- `ha.tx_push_factor`: Amount of slaves the master will try to push to a transaction before returning success to client. We can also set this to `0`, which will switch off the synchronous data writes to the slave node and would eventually increase the write performance. However, this would also increase the risk of data loss, as the master would be the only node containing the transaction.

- `ha.tx_push_strategy`: This should be either `fixed` or `round_robin`. It means the priority of nodes, which will be selected to push the events. In the case of `fixed`, the priority is decided based on the value of `ha.server_id`, which is further based on the principle of highest first.

All write transaction on a slave will be first synchronized with the master. When the transaction commits, it will be first committed on the master and, if successful, then it will be committed on the slave. To ensure consistency, the slave has to be updated and synchronized with the master before performing a write operation. This is built into the communication protocol between the slave and master, so that updates are applied automatically to a slave node communicating with its master node.

Neo4j provides the full data replication on each node, so that each node is self-sufficient to serve read and write requests. It also helps in achieving low latency. In order to serve a global audience, additional Neo4j servers can be configured as read-only slave servers and these servers can be placed near to the customer (may be geographically). These slave read-only servers are synced up with the master in real time and all local read requests are directed and served by these read-only slave servers, which provides data locality for our client applications.

Advanced settings

Let's discuss about the advanced settings exposed by Neo4j that should be considered for any production deployments.

`<$NEO4J_HOME>\conf\neo4j-server.properties`: Neo4j server configuration file:

Parameter	Default value	Description
`org.neo4j.server. webserver.address`	`0.0.0.0`	Client accept the pattern for the webserver. By default, it accepts connection only from local boxes. Defines IP address of the box for accepting remote connections. Defining it to `0.0.0.0` accepts connection from all addresses, not just from local boxes.
`org.neo4j.server. webserver.maxthreads`	`200`	Controlling the concurrent request handled by the webserver.
`org.neo4j.server. transaction.timeout`	`60`	Timeouts for orphaned transactions.

`<$NEO4J_HOME>\conf\neo4j.propoerties`: Low-level configurations for Neo4j database:

Parameter	Default value	Description
`Read_only`	`False`	Boolean value for enabling read mode or write mode. By default it is in write mode.
`Cache_type`	`Soft`	Defines the type of cache used to store the nodes and relationships: `none`: Do not use any cache. `soft`: LRU cache using soft references. Used when application load isn't very high. `weak`: LRU cache using weak references. Used when application is under heavy load with lots of reads and traversals. `strong`: Will hold on to all data that gets loaded and never release it. Use it when your graph is small enough to fit in memory. `hpc`: High-performance cache, which is only available with the Enterprise version of Neo4j.

Parameter	Default value	Description
dump_configuraton	False	Logs all configuration parameters at the time of server start up.
query_cache_size	100	Number of Cypher query execution plans to be cached.
keep_logical_logs	7 days	Logical transaction logs for being able to backup the database. It is used to specify the threshold to prune logical logs.
logical_log_ rotation_threshold	25M	Size of the file which will be used to auto-rotate the logical log file after a certain threshold. Value of 0 means there is no rotation based on size of file.

Apart from the previous properties, we can also configure and tune the JVM by defining the configurations such as type of GC, GC logs, max and min memory, and so on in <$NEO4J_HOME>\conf\neo4j-wrapper.conf.

In this section, we discussed about the physical layout of the Neo4j server and database. We also talked about setting up a high availability cluster and fault tolerant cluster.

Let's move forward and discuss the various monitoring options provided by Neo4j.

Monitoring the health of the Neo4J nodes

In this section, we will talk about the various aspects of monitoring exposed by Neo4j.

Neo4j browser

Neo4j exposes the REST endpoints which can be used to query the configuration of our server and database, and to make it simpler Neo4j Browser incorporates these REST endpoints and facilitates the execution of these REST endpoints in few clicks.

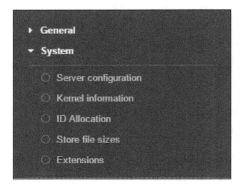

The previous screenshot shows the various options available in Neo4j Browser to query the configuration and health of your Neo4j database and server.

Webadmin

Webadmin was replaced with Neo4j Browser in Neo4j 2.0 release but it is still packaged and available. However, no enhancements or bug fixes are planned for the webadmin in upcoming releases.

You can still access webadmin by pointing your browser to `http://localhost:7474/webadmin` and you will see a nice dashboard providing high-level statistics. You can further explore and click on **Server Info** to get more information and statistics about your Neo4j database/server.

The following screenshot shows the dashboard displayed by webadmin:

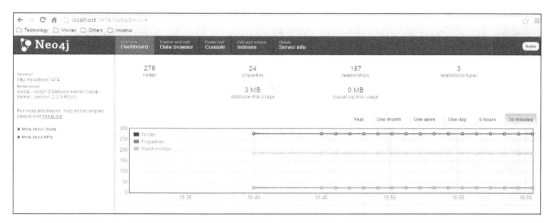

JMX beans

Neo4j Browser and webadmin are good tools for monitoring, but that is not enough for enterprise class systems, where we need detailed monitoring, statistics, and options to modify certain configuration at runtime without restarting the server.

Neo4j exposes JMX beans for advanced level of monitoring and management, which not only expose the overall health of our Neo4j server and database but also provide certain operations, which can be invoked over live Neo4j instance and that too without restarting the server. Most of the monitoring options exposed through JMX beans are only available with the Enterprise version of Neo4j.

 For more information on JMX, please refer to `http://www.oracle.com/technetwork/java/javase/tech/javamanagement-140525.html`.

Java provides JConsole (`http://docs.oracle.com/javase/7/docs/technotes/guides/management/jconsole.html`) which is packaged with standard JDK 7 distribution for viewing, modifying, and invoking the attributes or operations exposed by JMX beans. JConsole is also leveraged for viewing the overall health of our system where it exposes the various memory statistics such as heap, non-heap, threads JVM configurations, classes loaded in VM, and active threads and their current state.

Let's move forward and discuss the configurations required for enabling JMX beans via JConsole for viewing the various monitoring attributes exposed by Neo4j.

Perform the following steps to view JMX beans and JConsole in remote mode in Windows OS. For Linux, replace the forward slash \ with backward slash /; the remaining steps will remain the same.

1. Open `<$NEO4J_HOME>\conf\neo4j-wrapper.conf` and enable the following properties:

    ```
    wrapper.java.additional=-Dcom.sun.management.jmxremote.port=3637
    wrapper.java.additional=-Dcom.sun.management.jmxremote.
    authenticate=true
    wrapper.java.additional=-Dcom.sun.management.jmxremote.ssl=false
    wrapper.java.additional=-Dcom.sun.management.jmxremote.password.
    file=conf/jmx.password
    wrapper.java.additional=-Dcom.sun.management.jmxremote.access.
    file=conf/jmx.access
    ```

    All the preceding properties define the configuration of JMX beans, such as communication port, username and password files, and so on.

2. Next we need to modify the username and password for connecting JMX server remotely. Open `<$NEO4J_HOME>\conf\jmx.access` and uncomment the line `control readwrite`. Uncommenting this line will enable the admin role for the JMX beans and you can modify and invoke the operations exposed by Neo4j JMX beans.

3. Now we will add username and password in `jmx.password`. Open `<$NEO4J_HOME>\conf\jmx.password` and, at the end of the file, enter `control <space><password>` like `control Sumit`, where the first word is the username and second is the password. Username should match with the entry made in the `jmx.access` file.

4. We also need to make sure that the permissions for `conf\jmx.password` is `0600` in Linux. Open the console and execute `sudo chmod 0600 conf\jmx.password` in Linux, and for Windows follow the instructions defined at `http://docs.oracle.com/javase/7/docs/technotes/guides/management/security-windows.html`.

5. In your Windows console, execute `<$JAVA_HOME>\bin\jconsole` and select **Remote Process**. In the text box, enter `localhost:3637`, the username as `control` and the password as `Sumit`.

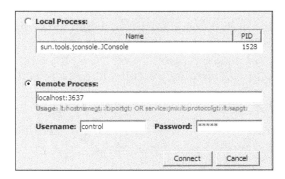

And we are done! Click on **Connect** and you will be able to see the UI of JConsole exposing the health statistics of your system along with the MBeans exposed by Neo4j.

The following screenshot shows the various management beans exposed by Neo4j:

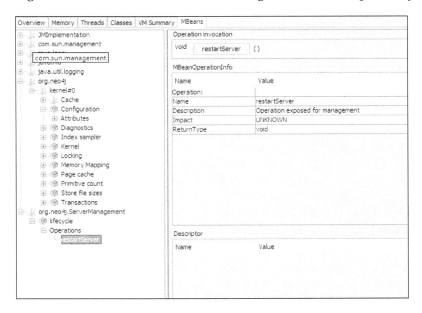

In this section, we discussed about the various options and tools available for monitoring our Neo4j server and database. Let's move forward and discuss other enterprise concerns such as backup and recovery.

Backup and recovery

In this section, we will talk about options available for performing backups and restoring Neo4j database.

Backup and recovery is another challenge for distributed systems. Neo4j provides tools and utilities for performing online backup and recovery, which is in sync with the enterprise operational needs. It provides `<$NEO4J_HOME>\bin\neo4j-backup` as a command-line utility for performing the full and incremental/hot backups.

The following steps need to be performed to enable backups:

- **Enabling online backup**: `online_backup_enabled` should be enabled in `<$NEO4J_HOME>\conf\neo4j.properties`.

- **Full backup**: Create a blank directory on the machine where you want to take the full backup and run the following backup tool:

  `<$NEO4J_HOME>\bin\neo4j-backup -host <IP-ADDRESS> -port <PORT#> -to <DIR location on remote server>`.

- **Incremental backup**: Run the same command that we used to take the full backup and `neo4j-backup` will only copy the updates from the last backup. Incremental backups can fail when the provided directory does not have a valid backup or if the previous backup is from the older version of Neo4j database.

 Refer to `http://neo4j.com/docs/stable/backup-introduction.html` for more information on backups in Neo4j.

- **Recovering database from backup**: Modify the `org.neo4j.server.database.location` property in `<$NEO4J_HOME>\conf\neo4j-server.properties` and provide the location of the directory where the backup is stored, and restart your Neo4j server. Depending upon the size of your data, it may take some time but eventually it will be up-and-running within few minutes.

 Refer to `http://neo4j.com/docs/stable/backup-restoring.html` for more information on restoring the Neo4j database from backups.

Summary

In this chapter, we learned and discussed about the various production deployment aspects of Neo4j, such as physical and logical architecture, file layouts, and data organization on the physical devices, monitoring, and backup and recovery.

Index

Cypher queries
  basic anatomy 24
  running 129, 130
Cypher query, optimizations
  about 58, 64-66
  execution plan 62, 63
  indexes 59-61
  index, sampling 61

D

database files 136
Database Management System (DBMS) 45
data types, Cypher
  reference link 30
delete operation 32
Dijkstra algorithm
  about 141
  URL 141
Django
  Neomodel, using 130, 131
  signals, URL 115
  URL 115, 130, 131

E

Enterprise Edition
  Enterprise subscriptions 9
  personal license 8
  startup program 9
execution phases, Cypher
  about 25
  execution plan 25
  initial node(s), locating 26
  parsing 25
  plan, analyzing 62, 63
  relationships, selecting 26
  relationships, traversing 26
  validating 25
  values, modifying 26
  values, returning 26
ext4 filesystem
  reference link 135
extensions, Flask
  reference link 95

Extreme Programming
  URL 88

F

fault tolerance 144
Flask
  about 93
  installing 94, 95
  URL 93, 97
Flask application
  about 96
  creating, steps 96, 97
  dynamic content, displaying 99, 100
  static content, displaying 98, 99
Flask RESTful API
  about 101
  creating, steps 101, 102
  JSON Processing 102-104

G

Garbage Collector (GC) 138
general clauses
  limit clause 37
  order by clause 37
  skip clause 37
  UNION ALL clause 38
  UNION clause 38
  using, with patterns 36
  WITH clause 37, 38
General Public License (GPL)
  URL 8
GitHub
  URL 68
Graph API
  URL 71
graph models, components
  about 2
  labels 6
  nodes 5
  properties 6
  relationship 6
graphs 23
Gremlin
  URL 24

features 142
high availability 142, 143
Neo4j REST interface
about 16
authentication 16, 17
authorization 16
CRUD operations 17-19
Neo4j shell
options 14
using 14, 15
Neomodel
configuring 116-118
installing 116-118
nodes, defining 118, 119
properties, defining 119-121
PyPI, URL 116
relationships, adding to models 125-128
signals 131
social data model, persisting 121-125
social data model, querying 121-125
URL 115, 132
using, in Django app 130
nodes
about 46
constraints, working with 56
CREATE UNIQUE clause 55
defining 118, 119
label, updating 58
MERGE clause, creating 56
multiple nodes 48
properties, updating 57
single node 46, 47
unique nodes, creating 55
with full paths 55
with labels 48, 49
with properties 49, 50
working with 39-43
Non-Functional Requirements (NFRs) 133

O

Object Graph Mapper (OGM)
URL 115
Object Relational Model (ORM)
about 105
for graph databases py2neo 105
online transaction processing (OLTP) 1

OPTIONALMATCH statement 28
Oracle Java 7
URL, for download 9, 12
order by clause 37

P

Path API
URL 83
patterns
about 32
for labels 34
for nodes 34
for properties 35
for relationships 34, 35
general clauses, using with 36
pattern matching 32
using, in where clause 36
where clause, using with 35
Paxos
reference link 144
physical architecture, Neo4j
about 142
advanced settings 146
data locality 145
data replication 145
fault tolerance 144
high availability 142, 143
PIP
URL 69
pre-built algorithms, for graph traversals
A* 141
all paths 140
all simple paths 140
Dijkstra 141
shortest path 140
probabilistic model 2
properties
data types 50
defining 119-121
nodes with 49, 50
relationships with 54
URL 120
py2neo
Batch imports 86, 87
configuring 68
installing 68-70

prerequisites 68, 69
used, for creating social network 83-86
py2neo APIs
Authentication API 71, 72
Cypher queries 77-79
Graph API 70, 71
Node class 72-75
Paths 81, 82
Relationship class 75-77
transactions 80, 81
PyPy
URL 67
pytest
URL 91
Python
about 67, 94
URL 68, 115
Python Package Index (PPI) 68
Python Packaging Authority (PYPA) 69

R

race condition
reference link 133
read operations
about 27, 135
AGGREGATION 29
MATCH 27, 28
OPTIONALMATCH 28
START 28, 29
record files 135-137
recovery 152
relational models 2
relationships
about 51
adding, to models 125-128
multiple relationships 52-54
single relationship 51, 52
unique relationships, creating 55
updating 58
with full paths 55
with properties 54
working with 39-43
remove operation 32

Representational State Transfer (REST) API
about 93, 141
for social network data, py2neo 104
URL 20, 141

S

sample dataset
creating, steps 33, 34
Service Level Agreements (SLAs) 133
SET operation 31
shortest path algorithm
about 140
reference link 140
Sinatra Ruby framework
URL 94
skip clause 37
social data model, Neomodel
persisting 121-125
querying 121-125
social network
creating, py2neo used 83-86
social network application, with Flask-RESTful and OGM
about 106
object model, creating 106-110
REST APIs, creating over data model 110-114
SQL
and Cypher, comparing 3-5
and graph databases, similarities 2
SQL alike 25
SQL developers
graphs, using 2
SQL models
graph structures, evolving from 5-7
standard deviation 29
START query 28, 29

T

Test Drive Development (TDD)
URL 88
Transactional Cypher HTTP Endpoint 20

transaction logs
  about 137
  reference link 137
transaction management
  principles 45
traversal framework 140

U

UNION ALL clause 38
UNION clause 38
unit testing 88-91
update operation 30

V

values, cache_type parameter
  Hpc 139
  None 139
  Soft 139
  Strong 139
  Weak 139

W

webadmin
  about 148
  URL, for accessing 148
web applications
  setting up, with Flask 96
  setting up, with Flask-RESTful 96
Werkzeug
  URL 94
where clause
  patterns, using in 36
  using, with patterns 35
WITH clause 37, 38
write operation 135

Z

ZFS
  reference link 135

Thank you for buying
Building Web Applications with Python and Neo4j

About Packt Publishing

Packt, pronounced 'packed', published its first book, *Mastering phpMyAdmin for Effective MySQL Management*, in April 2004, and subsequently continued to specialize in publishing highly focused books on specific technologies and solutions.

Our books and publications share the experiences of your fellow IT professionals in adapting and customizing today's systems, applications, and frameworks. Our solution-based books give you the knowledge and power to customize the software and technologies you're using to get the job done. Packt books are more specific and less general than the IT books you have seen in the past. Our unique business model allows us to bring you more focused information, giving you more of what you need to know, and less of what you don't.

Packt is a modern yet unique publishing company that focuses on producing quality, cutting-edge books for communities of developers, administrators, and newbies alike. For more information, please visit our website at www.packtpub.com.

About Packt Open Source

In 2010, Packt launched two new brands, Packt Open Source and Packt Enterprise, in order to continue its focus on specialization. This book is part of the Packt Open Source brand, home to books published on software built around open source licenses, and offering information to anybody from advanced developers to budding web designers. The Open Source brand also runs Packt's Open Source Royalty Scheme, by which Packt gives a royalty to each open source project about whose software a book is sold.

Writing for Packt

We welcome all inquiries from people who are interested in authoring. Book proposals should be sent to author@packtpub.com. If your book idea is still at an early stage and you would like to discuss it first before writing a formal book proposal, then please contact us; one of our commissioning editors will get in touch with you.

We're not just looking for published authors; if you have strong technical skills but no writing experience, our experienced editors can help you develop a writing career, or simply get some additional reward for your expertise.

Learning Neo4j

ISBN: 978-1-84951-716-4   Paperback: 222 pages

Run blazingly fast queries on complex graph datasets with the power of the Neo4j graph database

1. Get acquainted with graph database systems and apply them in real-world use cases.

2. Get started with Neo4j, a unique NoSQL database system that focuses on tackling data complexity.

3. A practical guide filled with sample queries, installation procedures, and useful pointers to other information sources.

Learning Cypher

ISBN: 978-1-78328-775-8   Paperback: 162 pages

Write powerful and efficient queries for Neo4j with Cypher, its official query language

1. Improve performance and robustness when you create, query, and maintain your graph database.

2. Save time by writing powerful queries using pattern matching.

3. Step-by-step instructions and practical examples to help you create a Neo4j graph database using Cypher.

Please check **www.PacktPub.com** for information on our titles

www.ingramcontent.com/pod-product-compliance
Lightning Source LLC
LaVergne TN
LVHW081343050326
832903LV00024B/1278